THE
ACTS OF PILATE

and

ANCIENT RECORDS RECORDED BY CONTEMPORARIES OF JESUS CHRIST REGARDING THE FACTS CONCERNING HIS BIRTH, DEATH, RESURRECTION

Originally Titled:
THE
ARCHKO VOLUME

OR, THE
Archeological Writings of the Sanhedrim
And Talmuds of the Jews

TRANSLATED BY
DRS. McINTOSH and TWYMAN

Compiled and Edited by
REV. W. D. MAHAN

The Acts of Pilate, Edited Rev. W.D. Mahan
ISBN # 089-228-127-8

Copyright, ©, 1997
IMPACT CHRISTIAN BOOKS, INC.
332 Leffingwell Ave.,
Kirkwood, MO 63122

Cover Design: Niki Blake

ALL RIGHTS RESERVED

PRINTED IN THE UNITED STATES OF AMERICA

Originally entitled, *THE ARCHKO VOLUME*,
Entered according to Act of Congress, in the year 1887, by
REV. W. D. MAHAN
in the Office of the Librarian of Congress, at Washington, D.C.

CONTENTS

	PAGE
Foreword	*v*
Publisher's Preface	*vii*

CHAPTER I.
How these records were discovered   1

CHAPTER II.
A short sketch of the Talmuds   39

CHAPTER III.
Constantine's letter in regard to having fifty copies of the Scriptures written and bound   46

CHAPTER IV.
Jonathan's interview with the Bethlehem shepherds--Letter of Melker, Priest of the Synagogue at Bethlehem   50

CHAPTER V.
Gamaliel's interview with Joseph and Mary and others concerning Jesus   63

CHAPTER VI.
Report of Caiaphas to the Sanhedrim concerning the execution of Jesus   79

CHAPTER VII.
Report of Caiaphas to the Sanhedrim concerning the resurrection of Jesus   97

CHAPTER VIII.
Valleus's notes – "*Acta Pilati*," or **Pilate's report to Caesar** of the arrest, trial, and crucifixion of Jesus — 107

CHAPTER IX.
Herod Antipater's defence before the Roman Senate in regard to his conduct at Bethlehem.. — 126

CHAPTER X.
Herod Antipas's defence before the Roman Senate in regard to the execution of John the Baptist — 132

CHAPTER XI.
The Hillel letters regarding God's providence to the Jews, by Hillel the Third — 137

FOREWORD

I have been searching and praying for the little book you have in your hands right now, for more than thirty years. As a direct answer to prayer God brought it to me.

Each year at Easter time Kathryn Kuhlman would read the account of Jesus Christ written as a court document. I would sit glued to the radio, as I listened to Miss Kuhlman read the account of the birth, death and resurrection of Jesus, and the rest of the account recorded by Caiaphas, the man the who killed Jesus. I would cry about my Savior's death and rejoice with His resurrection as the stone was rolled away.

I dearly wanted to have this little book which has so much written on a few pages, but never knew where to find it. I thought to myself that was just one of the many treasures which God had given to Miss Kuhlman.

After her death, I went to the man who inherited all her possessions and begged him for just two things: a dark brown sweater she wore each day as she taped the message for the radio program and this little book. He denied my request, and so I prayed that God would somehow give me this precious and very special book as a gift.

Years and years and years went by. Even though I had forgotten my request of my God, He had not. One evening recently while sitting in a meeting in St. Louis, Mo, the guest evangelist said, "Ask God to bring to you any request you have made in the past that has not yet become a reality to you. Even if it has been a long time, just raise your hands and ask Him to bring it to you."

I quickly raised my hands and thought and prayed, "God, I can t even remember what I have asked for, so, please bring to me those things that I have asked for, but have not yet seen come to pass. God, I know You have heard my prayers."

I thanked Him and the service ended. I began talking with my husband and the folks I had brought to the service. Suddenly, a young lady came and stood in front of me. She said she was in St. Louis from Florida, and didn't know why, but *God had been showing her my face for three days.* We chatted for a few moments, then she said good-bye and became lost in the crowd. I never expected to see her again.

Later that night I was among the last to leave the church and again, suddenly, the young lady appeared. She said she remembered my making a comment about Lazarus and wanted to give me a book she had about Lazarus, and the death and resurrection of Jesus.

My heart leaped inside me, as I remembered my request years earlier, and I knew it was *the book.* Oh, my dear God in Heaven, it must be THE BOOK!

I ran with her to her car which, she had left in the church parking lot, heading the wrong direction, with the lights on and motor running, as she had started to leave and then been directed back. She opened the door and handed the little book to me.

It was, indeed, **the book I had prayed for thirty years earlier**, after my own healing. **Our God never forgets. Our prayers are always answered**.

I pray this little book will bless you as it has me. God bless you.

Joan Gieson,
Joan Gieson Ministries, St. Louis, Mo.

Formerly associated with Kathryn Kuhlman for eight and one-half years, running the Midwestern Foundation office in Missouri.

Associated with Benny Hinn Crusades for the past six years, praying for the sick.

PUBLISHER'S PREFACE

Having operated a retail Christian Bookstore for more than twenty-five years, I had never heard of, nor can I recall a single customer ever inquiring about this volume. So it has managed to remain largely hidden from the view of the majority of Christendom since it was first published in 1887. Perhaps part of the reason that the book has attracted so little attention is due to its having been self-published and to its original title, *The Archko Volume*, which sheds little light upon the contents.

No doubt part of the reason the original records, which Rev. Mahan consulted, lay undiscovered for so many years is a result of the doctrine of *Sola Scriptura*– the belief that a true Christian needs nothing in addition to the Scripture. While it is certainly true that we do not need extra-biblical proof for our faith, on the other hand, our faith is certainly not diminished, when scientific knowledge happens to confirm Biblical truths, such as when it was discovered that the earth is round, or that there are fish capable of swallowing a man alive.

We have presented in this volume, the work as originally edited and compiled by Rev. W. D. Mahan, without attempting to correct any of the spelling ("to-day" "defence") which was in vogue at the time of writing. We have also maintained his punctuation (or lack of it) and the rather unique spacing employed with colons, semi-colons and question marks. Some of his paragraphs are longer, and many of his sentences could be more easily grasped had commas been more liberally used. However, I think you will discover this volume to be such a treasure, and such a confirmation to your faith that differences in language and punctuation will melt away.

Another point that will no doubt come to mind is how can we be sure that these records are authentic and accurately translated. I can say that in twenty-seven years of Bible study and teaching, I have only in recent years found certain facts which are presented in this book. For example, it was only in the last year or so that I ran across an old commentary which revealed one of the truths mentioned herein, that Pilate had only *one hundred Roman Soldiers at his disposal* at the time of the crucifixion. It is also interesting to notice that the Jews at the time of Christ had a practice of interviewing potential candidates for Messiahship, as is recorded in the case of John the Baptist (John 1:19-28).

I have felt a great kinship with Rev. Mahan for he and I have more in common than our initials. We both have attempted to serve the Lord as ministers, in the State of Missouri, we both were drawn by Divine Providence to devote ten years to researching "lost topics" recorded in secular history, which were confirmations of Christianity. We both traveled to great libraries in foreign countries in search of material. Afterward, we both wrote a book detailing the results of our searches, his, of course, the book in your hand, *The Acts of Pilate* (originally entitled *The Archko Volume*) and mine *The Heavens Declare...*, published almost one hundred years apart, in 1887 and 1985.

I have personally been blessed by this little book, and my prayer is that it will bless you, and those with whom you will share it.

W.D. BANKS,
Kirkwood, Mo.
August, 1997

CHAPTER 1.

HOW THESE RECORDS WERE DISCOVERED.

Sometime in the year 1856, while living in De Witt, Missouri, a gentleman by the name of H. C. Whydaman became snow-bound and stopped at my house several days. He was a native of Germany, and one of the most learned men I had ever met. I found him to be freely communicative. During his stay, he told me he had spent five years in the city of Rome, and most of the time in the Vatican, where he saw a library containing five hundred and sixty thousand volumes. He told me that he had seen and read the records of Tiberius Caesar, and in what was called the *Acta Pilati* – that is, the acts of Pilate – he had seen an account of the apprehension, trial, and crucifixion of Jesus of Nazareth; but said it did not add much to the commonly accepted teachings of Christianity. He told me he thought a transcript could be secured. After Mr. Whydaman's departure, I meditated upon what he had told me of those records, and thought that if a transcript could be obtained it would be very interesting, even if it did not add much to the present teachings of Christianity So, after some months I set about tracing up Mr. Whydaman, as the following correspondence shows:

DEWITT, CARROLL CO., Mo., Sept. 22, 1856.
MR. HENRY C. WHYDAMAN.

DEAR SIR: After you left my house last spring, I kept thinking of your telling me of reading the acts of Pilate in the Vatican, while at Rome. I want you, if you please, to get me a transcript of those records, if the cost will not be too much. Will you please open a correspondence with some of your old friends at Rome that you can rely upon, and ascertain if it can be obtained; and if so what will be the probable cost of getting it? I shall be much obliged, and will pay you for your trouble and expense.

Yours in tender regards,
W. D. MAHAN.

NEW YORK, Nov. 12, 1856,

MR. W. D. MAHAN.

DEAR SIR: Your letter as directed to H. C. Whydaman is received. I will inform you he has returned to Germany. Your letter has been forwarded.

Yours, etc.,
C.C. VANTBERGER.

March 2, 1857.

REV. W. D. MAHAN.

DEAR SIR: It is with the kindest regards I remembered your hospitality while with you in America. Be assured, anything I can do for you will afford me great pleasure. I have written to Father Freelinhusen, a monk of great learning, at Rome, who is the chief guardian of the Vatican. I have made the request in my own name, as I do not think they would be willing for such a document to go into the hands of the public. When he answers, I will write to you again.

I am, your most obedient servant,
H. C. WHYDAMAN.

WESTPHALIA, GERMANY, Nov. 27, 1857.
REV. W. D. MAHAN.

DEAR SIR: Father Freelinhusen has answered my letter in regard to the transcript you want. He informs me that the writing is so fine, and being in the Latin language, as I told you, and the parchments so old and dirty, he will be obliged to use a glass to the most of it. He can only give it in the Latin, as he does not understand the English. He says he will do it for thirty-five darics, which will be in American coin sixty-two dollars and forty-four cents. If you will forward the amount, I will have the document forwarded to my brother-in-law, C. C. Vantberger. He will translate it for a trifle.

I am yours, in tender regards.
H. C. WHYDAMAN.

CHILLICOTHE, Mo., Feb. 8, 1858.
MR. H. C. WHYDAMAN.

DEAR SIR: Thanks to you for your kindness, and be assured, if I succeed, I shall ever feel under obligations to you for your trouble. Enclosed find a check on the Foreign Exchange Bank of New York for sixty-two dollars and forty-four cents. Please have the work done, and urge Mr. Freelinhusen to have it a true copy of the original. Send it to Mr. Vantberger, and have him to translate it into English, and I will pay the charges. He has my address.

Yours, as ever,
W. D. MAHAN.

WESTPHALIA, GERMANY, June 14, 1858.
REV. W. D. MAHAN.
   DEAR SIR: I acknowledge your draft of $62.44. Will apply as you request.
                    I am, sir,
                       H. C. WHYDAMAN.

MR. H. C. WHYDAMAN.
   DEAR SIR: I hereby forward to you the transcript as it is on record in the Vatican in Tiberius Caesar's Court by Pilate. I certify this to be a true copy, word for word, as it occurs there.
                    Yours, etc.,
                       PETER FREELINHUSEN.

                               NEW YORK, April 26,1859.
MR. W. D. MAHAN.
   DEAR SIR : I am in possession of a document from H. C. Whydaman, with instructions to translate it into English. My charge is ten dollars. I will expect an answer.
                       C. C. VANTBERGER.

   With this correspondence I received the following document, and I must confess that, although it is not inspired, yet the words burned in my heart as the words of Christ in the hearts of his disciples, and I am satisfied from the spirit it breathes that it must be true. I am aware that though the Jews were in subjection to the Romans, yet they still held their ecclesiastical authority, and the Romans not only submitted to their decisions, but executed their decrees on their subjects. Knowing there was not such a piece of history to be found in all the world, and being deeply interested myself, as also

DISCOVERY OF THE RECORDS 5

hundreds of others to whom I have read it, I have concluded to give it to the public.

Upon getting hold of this report of Pilate I commenced to investigate this subject, and after many years of trial and the expenditure of considerable money, I found that there were many of such records still preserved at the Vatican in Rome and at Constantinople, that had been carried there by the Emperor of Rome about the middle of the third century. I therefore procured the necessary assistance, and on September 21, 1883, I set sail for those foreign lands to make the investigation in person.

Believing that no event of such importance to the world as the death of Jesus of Nazareth could have transpired without some record being made of it by his enemies in their courts, legislations, and histories, I commenced investigating the subject. After many years of study, and after consulting various histories and corresponding with many scholars, I received the assistance of two learned men, Drs. McIntosh and Twyman, and went to the Vatican at Rome, and then to the Jewish Talmuds at Constantinople. As a result I have compiled this book, which will be found one of the most strange and interesting books ever read. It may appear fragmentary, but the reader must remember that it is the record of men made nearly two thousand years ago.

It was some time in March, 1856, that my mind was awakened on the subject of this book, almost incidentally, or it may be providentially, for He sometimes chooses the weakest things to confound the mighty. The reader is referred to the correspondence of H. C. Whydaman and myself, as found in this book. In

God's providence sometimes very great effects are produced from very small causes. Mr. Whydaman told me he had spent five years in the Vatican at Rome, and in looking over the old manuscripts he came across the records of Pilate made to Caesar, and in those records he saw where a man named Jesus was arrested, tried, and executed; he read it carefully and re-read it, and went back and read it again.

This was the beginning of my investigation, and this book is the product of that investigation. I ask the reader to follow me patiently and see how I came to get hold of the matter contained in this book.

I wondered how it was that such historians as Philo, Tacitus, Quintilian, and Josephus had told us nothing or so little about Jesus of Nazareth. I asked all the wise men and scholars I met, and they did not know; I then wrote to many scholars in Europe, and they could not tell me. As I could find nothing very definite from the outside world, I began to have my doubts, but came to the conclusion that the question was of too much importance to allow my mind to be fixed without a thorough investigation. I went to our histories—Mosheim, Lardner, Stackhouse, and others. They gave me no satisfaction, and I thought to myself, Is it possible that the character of such men as the early Christians, and the wonderful excitement that they created in their day, could have been passed over and no records made of them? When I remembered, too, that the Roman provinces in that day were prolific with debaters, historians, and writers on all topics that were brought before them, and that the records of the courts in those days were more carefully preserved than they are now, and that even of the trial of Guiteau, who was not half as conspicuous to the people of these United States as Jesus was to the Jewish nation, there were hundreds of records made, I came to the conclusion that only Almighty God could establish a cause so universally as the Christian religion was established in the hearts of the people of this world, and sceptre them so completely as the sceptre of Jesus governs this world today, when they had comparatively little or no testimony from the outside world.

I consulted our histories in this country, and one said these records were burned in the Alexandrian Library. I knew the Babylonian Talmuds were in this library, or at least most of them were, but I also knew that the Talmuds of Jerusalem were not. I knew that when the Romans conquered the Jews and destroyed their Holy City, temple and all, all the sacred Treasures were taken by the Romans and, I supposed, preserved.

Another historian says Gregory IX. burned all the sacred records. I found that this Roman bishop was a strong believer in Christ, as were all the Catholic Church. They follow not us, and we forbid them. Why should they burn these records? There is no Church more strongly in favor of Jesus Christ; he is their corner-stone, their foundation rock, their only hope. They have a different way to approach him. This does not destroy their Saviour; he remains the same, but they have different ways of using him as their Saviour.

Other historians said the Jews destroyed these records, although it is strange that the Jews should destroy all their sacred records at the time, to get rid of an impostor, as they believed him to be. It is more likely they would have preserved them to vindicate their actions in the future, provided they should be needed. The Jews were honest in all their dealings with Christ; they thought both he and John the Baptist were destroying their nation, and, as their nation and religion were one and the same, the course Jesus was pursuing jeopardized all their hopes, religious and political. This is seen clearly in the defence of Caiaphas, as set forth in this book (see his defence before the Sanhedrim in regard to his conduct with Jesus). Hence, much of the prejudice among Protestants against the Jews is groundless. There never was a people more honest and devoted to their country and their God than the Jews. Many Protestants in this country, and some preachers among them, think that the more they denounce the Jews and Catholics, the more they serve God. The Jews were wrong in rejecting Jesus Christ as their Saviour, and so are those who reject him now; but when a man reads this book he will come to the conclusion that the Jews had a better reason for rejecting Christ than men have today, and would it be right to abuse all who refuse Christ as bad men ? It is still more intolerable for the members of one denomination to abuse those of another because of not worshipping Christ as they do.

A difficulty I met in consulting scholars on this subject was the claim that the Roman monks had forged many manuscripts regarding Jesus Christ, in the middle ages. Now they may have forged some things to sustain their peculiar views and doctrines, something to sustain their Church ; but there is nothing in this book to sustain Catholicism, and if every word of it was forgotten it would add nothing to that Church more than to any other

Church. Then I remembered the Vatican library was one of the most extensive in the world ; it has cost millions of dollars. How did those forgers know that I or any other man would come there and pay them a few dollars to get a transcript of those records ? It certainly would be a very poor speculation.

Another objection was that the manuscripts had been searched for by scholars and could not be found. So I set myself to work, and after investigating all the authors in this country, and writing to many scholars in Europe, and getting books from libraries in the old country, thus sparing no pains or expense, I could not find or even hear of a man who had ever investigated this subject. I found that Dr. Tischendorf made some investigation in these ancient manuscripts, but he was looking for the manuscript of the Scriptures, and might have seen many such things as this book holds and never have noticed them, just from the simple fact that he was not looking for them. He was looking for something else. In the investigation of such subjects a man must have but one thing in his mind, and he must be posted beforehand to know how and where to look, for the field is too large to make his business general. I now challenge any scholar to show me the man who has made this his special business, and made the effort that I have on this particular subject. I am sure there is none.

The next great difficulty that I encountered was this: Could such manuscripts exist so long? I found by investigating that Ptolemy, King of Alexandria, presented seventy books to Ezra, which he refused to place in the Holy Canon, and it came very near bringing on a bloody war. Again I found that Serenus Samnaticus, who was the teacher of M. Antonius Africanus, son of Gordianus the Great, when he died, left his library, consisting of sixty-two thousand volumes, to his student. This was in 236 A.D. I also remembered that the works of Homer were more than five hundred years older than Christ, and that we had the laws of Shammai, Abtalian, and the works of the Hillels all before us; and if Tischendorf, in the convent of St. Catherine, could find slips and pieces of the Septuagint that were declared at Leipsic to be of the fourth century, I thought there might be a great deal more somewhere in the vast libraries in those old countries that have thousands of years the advantage of America. The literati could all tell how the manuscripts of the Church might be, and were, preserved; but the records of its enemies, even the records of courts and crowns they could not see into.

Now the reader must remember that there never was anything that created so much excitement in the land of Judea as the preaching of John the Baptist and Christ. This will be readily understood if we take into consideration the structure of the Jewish Commonwealth. The great Sanhedrim legislated for the souls and bodies of men; that is, their religion and their politics were one and the same thing. In the capitulation made with Augustus Caesar it was understood and agreed that the Jews were to pay a tax to the Romans, but the Romans were not to interfere with the Jewish religion. This took the executive power out of the hands of the Jews and put it into the hands of the Romans. This is the reason Jesus was sent to Pilate to be executed. The Romans had to carry out and execute the decisions of the Jewish courts on all Jewish questions. This is the reason Herod

Antipas was tried by the Roman Senate: he had executed John the Baptist without a trial. Then we see why the Jews and Romans worked together on all questions of law; hence the great excitement of both nations. This is the reason why Pilate made his report to Caesar. Now I say no event creating so much excitement could take place without more or less record being made of it; for if the Scripture is true–and I believe it is–there never was a man on earth who had so many followers in so short a time. Caiaphas says Jesus had been preaching three years, and he then had more followers than Abraham. This causes me to say again that if the New Testament records are true, then the historical items contained in this book must be true ; and if these items, or items like them, be not true, then the items of the New Testament are not true; that is, no man dare to say these are the identical items, but items like these, and why not these? They came from the right place. The parchments and scrolls upon which they are written are such as were used in those days, but to say these are the same is to say what no man dare to say. The time has been too long and the distance to the place where the records are kept is too great for all men to make the examination for themselves, hence I ask all to consider this question fairly.

Let me invite the attention of the reader to the known histories in this country. Dr. Rashi, D.D., who wrote in Paris in the twelfth century, says in Vol. III., page 190, that in the formation of the ancient libraries there were men appointed called "baalie suphoths," which means "book-compilers." The business of these men was to take the sheets of parchment of the various authors and pin their dates together, bind them in bundles and have them bound with clasps between cedar boards. This was a trade, and it required the best of scholars to do it. They were called baalie suphoths. We find that the works of Philo were compiled by Pseudonymaus Joseph Ben Gorion, A.D. 150. This Ben Gorion was a Jewish rabbi, a Pharisean doctor. Josephus was compiled by Ekaba, another Jewish doctor, at the close of the second century; and so with all the historians who lived near the Christian era. Josephus was published in book-form by Havercamp, in Amsterdam, in 1729. Now all he had to guide him was what Ben Gorion had said. So it is with Philo, which was put in book-form by Mangey, in London, in 1742 ; all he had was what Ekaba had pleased to compile of his works, and, as there was deadly hatred between Jews and Christians at that time, it is most reasonable to believe that those compilers would leave everything out that would favor the Christians. It was to their own interest at that time to bury the very name of Christ in eternal oblivion and this is the reason that all the historians who lived and wrote in those days are made to say so very little about Christ or his followers.

Now in looking over the histories we find comparatively nothing said about Jesus Christ. Such a thing could not be if the New Testament is true. No man could make me believe that such events occurred as are recorded in the Scriptures without accounts of them being made in the State records and by the public writers of that day. Although I have had this thrown in my face so often by infidels, I never saw the reason till I commenced this investigation; and if any man will take the pains to examine this question he will find that all the sophers, or scribes, were Pharisees; they were the doctors, lawyers, orators, poets, and statesmen of the times. The Hillel and Shammai schools made more scholars than all the world besides in the last days of the Jewish Commonwealth. Almost every nation under the sun patronized these schools.

Now, being satisfied that I was on the right track, the next thing was to find out what had become of the original manuscripts. Had Rothgad, Havercamp, and Mangey destroyed the manuscripts when they were done with them ? This I knew could not be, from the fact that these parchments were either in the hands of government or individual libraries, and they could not destroy them or take them away; and I knew if these manuscripts had been kept till 1754 they must be in existence yet. Only a few years ago there were one hundred and twenty-eight volumes of manuscripts presented to the British Museum, which were looked upon with interest, and, while I am writing this, there comes to my hand a dispatch from Vienna to the London Times. I will give it in full, as I think it will be beneficial to the reader. The dispatch is as follows:

"*Ancient Manuscripts.* The sifting and arrangement of the papyrus collection bought by Archduke Rainer have led to further interesting discoveries. Of the hieroglyphic, hieratic, demotic, and Coptic papyri, about twenty date from the pre-Christian period. Among these is one nearly three thousand years old, in the hieratic letter, containing the representation of a funeral, with a well-preserved sketch of the deceased, some hieroglyphic legends, and a demotic papyrus on the subject of mathematics. Much more numerous are the Coptic documents, about one thousand in all, mostly letters and legal documents of the period from the sixth to the tenth century of our era. There are some important papyri containing translations of the Bible in the central Egyptian dialect, of which there have hitherto been found but few specimens; and a leaf of parchment from an old octavo edition of the book of Ruth, in the Sahidi dialect.

"Among the Greek papyri is a hitherto unknown speech of Isocrates, one of the finest specimens of Alexandrian caligraphy. Another fragment has been found of the book of the Thucydides manuscript, previously mentioned. Portions, also, have been discovered of the Iliad, and a paraphrase of the Fourth Book. Then a metanvia has been found dating from the beginning of the fourth century, being thus one of the oldest Christian manuscripts. The collection contains many well-preserved documents in an almost continuous series of the Roman and Byzantine emperors, beginning with Trajan and ending with Heraclius.

"There are also documents in the Iranic and Semitic languages. The former are written on papyrus, parchment, and skins, and among them are two fragments which, it is believed, will furnish the key to the Pehlewi language. Among the Arab papyri twenty-five documents have been found with the original leaden seals attached. They begin with a fragment of the fifty-fourth year of the Hegira. Another is an official document of the nineteenth year of the Hegira, appointing a revenue collector. Perhaps the most valuable part of the collection is one hundred and fifty-five Arabian documents, on cotton paper, of the eighth century, which is about the time of the invention of this material by the

Arabs, to the year 953. Many thousands of manuscripts have still to be deciphered."

In the early centuries there was a good deal of what is known as the "Apologetical Writings." I made it my business to examine these writings, and found them to be a defence of Christianity. The first of this form of writing was presented to the Emperor Adrian by Quadratus, in the year 126 A.D. A portion of this we find in Eusebius, page 93. There was another by Aristides, at about the same time. These two authors are found only in fragments, preserved by other historians, and their writings are mainly pleas for clemency for those who professed Christianity and were being persecuted.

Justin Martyr also wrote twice on this subject—once to the Roman Senate and once to Antonius. These were published in English by W. Reeves, in 1709, at Leipsic.

Tertullian wrote two volumes, and Vincentius wrote a commentary on them. These are found at Paris. They are very valuable works—perhaps the most valuable of the ancient writings—from the fact, recorded in them, that the Christians, in giving reasons for asking favors, refer to the records made by the Jews and Jewish writers as well as the reports of the Roman officers who were the governors of Judea at that time; and of course their reference to these records demonstrates that the records were there.

In Tertullian, Vol. II., page 29, Vincentius says the Christians' argument was based on the doctrine of the Bible, showing that the God of the Christians could save, and referred the pagans to the many instances where he had interposed and saved, when none but a God like the

Christians' God could save. For, said they, what can a God made of wood or brass do in time of danger? They had no power to put forth and exert themselves to save. Vincentius says the pagan would answer that these images were the representations of their gods ; that these gods of wood and iron, had invisible spirits that exerted as much power as the God of the Christians. Vincentius says he did not see much difference in their doctrines when they got to understand each other.

I remember that, while on the ship, we had an Irish priest on board, and in conversation one day while asking him about many things in the Catholic Church I inquired why he had a crucifix hanging in his room. Said I, "You do not think there is any virtue in that image of brass?" "No," said he, "no more than there was in the serpent of brass that Moses made and placed on a pole. There were no healing virtues in that brass, but the bitten Israelite believed in the command, which belief or faith controlled his action and produced obedience; hence he was healed." And so, he said in this case, he no more believed there were any saving qualities in that image than I believe my mother's picture could be to me a mother.

Let the reader refer to the first centuries and mark what a disputation there was in the ancient church about pictures. May we not flow back into it? And as this subject of picture-worship created so much dissatisfaction in the first centuries it may do so again.

While investigating this question I found that Arcadius, the eldest son of Theodosius the Great, succeeded his father to the throne in A.D. 395, and divided the Roman Empire into what was known in that day as the Eastern and Western Empires.

DISCOVERY OF THE RECORDS 17

Arcadius chose the Eastern and fixed his seat of government at Constantinople, and made his brother Honorius Emperor of the Western, fixing his seat of government at Rome. It was not long until their jealously was kindled, which resulted in hatred and terminated in a war which finally proved their overthrow. In reading the Ante-Nicene Fathers, published in Edinburgh in twenty-four octavo volumes, in Vol. XII., page 114, it is said that the beginning of this war was on account of Honorius wishing to have his young princes educated at Constantinople free of charge, giving as his reason that the great library there had once belonged to Rome. When his brother Arcadius refused, he tried to get the library divided, and Arcadius refused this also. They then went to war, and while the two brothers were thus engaged Alaricus engaged the Western Empire and overthrew it. In hunting through this vast library of books I found what was called the Homilies of Clementine; Vol. XIII., page 194; there were the Apochryphal Gospels, Acts and Revelations, with all the writings of the Apostolic Fathers, including the laws of the High Priest, the laws of the Temple service, the Records of the Sanhedrim, giving the Jewish laws and customs for hundreds of years, with all the treaties and records of the courts.

Now my idea was that if these records were found in the library of the Vatican at Rome and in the Seraglio and Atmedan libraries at Constantinople and Alexandria, so these men could get them nearly three hundred years ago, why are they not there now?

Dr. Isaac Wise, who is President of the Hebrew School at Cincinnati, and, by the way, one of the best

Hebrew scholars in America, in his *History of the Commonwealth of Israel,* frequently quotes from the Talmuds and Sanhedrim, giving reference to the various circumstances, and often gives the name of the scribe who did the writing; and so I find these records have always been in the hands of the Jewish rabbis, and you need not tell me these things have been only produced by the later Jewish nation, for we find quotations made at the time and by the men who lived in the days of Christ. Those quotations correspond with other history we have of the same events, and the only difference is that the Jewish rabbis put a different construction on those events from what the Christians do. This is the great difficulty, after all; like a celebrated lawyer, after reading this book, told his friend it convinced him of the truth of the facts in the Scriptures, but it did not convince him of its spiritual definition. This is the final point of importance, when the soul is lost or saved—that is, to take the facts of the Scriptures and yield to them as spiritual truth. Colens the First, who was an Epicurean philosopher, wrote a treatise against Christianity and was answered by Origen. This work is in eight volumes. It was published in Paris, by Vallart, in 1746. In this work the disputants appealed alternately to these writings, to the reports made by the Romans, and show clearly that the whole of the Jewish doctrines, records and all, were then in possession of the Romans.

Nero refused to believe in these things, which he might have done if he had taken the pains to look into those sacred treasures of learning that were on file in the Senate chamber; but Origen says Nero was only moved by ambition, with the love of destruction before his eyes.

He never stopped to consider nor consult the opinions or wishes of others. Here, again, I found an unintentional reference to these things. Now the reader must remember that the records were there at that time, for no one disputed the fact; but in proving the unnecessary hostility of Nero, Origen makes mention of these other facts, showing the records to be in the city of Rome, how they came there, and what they taught; that is, a part of these records were brought from Jerusalem and were the writings of the Jews and the Romans who had been officers in the Jewish kingdom by Roman authority, and these were Roman officers, which made them a part of and responsible to the Roman government. Can any intelligent man believe that these men would have been allowed to transact the business of the Romans and no records be made of it in the archives of the government? Such a thing is most absurd. The reader will bear in mind that government among the Jews, Greeks, and Romans was much more strictly administered than in this country, and all such records as referred to the actions of the courts and the government officers had to be preserved. I now ask the attention of the reader to the investigation of the preservation of the sacred parchments from which come our Bible.

First, to the works of Benjamin Kennicott, D.D., entitled *Vetus Testamentum,* published in England in 1780. This is only a little more than one hundred years ago. We find that he got from the Codex of Hillel six hundred manuscripts. When did this Hillel live? The author of the Codex lived about one hundred years after the Christian era. Dr. Kennicott also got sixteen manuscripts from the Samaritan Pentateuch. Then I ask attention to John G. Rosenmueller, of 1736, at Leipsic, to his *Librarium*, five volumes, also his *Scholia Testament*, all from manuscript. Then to Brian Walton, D.D., born at Yorkshire in 1600, who published his polyglot Bible from manuscript (Hebrew). Because these are given to us by great men, and they suit our notions, they are never doubted ; and it is too apt to be the case in our *ad captandum*, we are not likely to investigate as closely as we should. And, again, we are apt to be more inclined to investigate those things that are suited to our tastes and interests; but while certain things are interesting to us we should never forget that there are other things equally interesting to others; and while we may be interested only in the sacred histories that make for our peace, and although the testimony of our enemies may not be very pleasant to hear, we should remember that the salvation of others may depend on such testimony.

We should not be opposed to any evidence that may give strength to any subject and thereby redound to good in a general way, specially if this evidence does not have a tendency to weaken our faith. It is so with this book ; it cannot weaken the faith of the Christian who has believed without foreign testimony, but brings strong corroborative testimony to enable others who are less credulous than we to believe. Hence in the examination of the various versions of the Bible and of the manner in which they were dug up out of the old manuscripts, from the rubbish of the ancient world, difficulties are encountered, and others may not believe as readily as we do. Duranzo, a Greek historian, who wrote thirty-six volumes in Constantinople at the close of the seventh and the beginning of the eighth century, in referring to the prosperity of the city and nation, says, in Vol. XIII., page 54, that Constantinople enjoyed educational advantages over all other cities, and that this was due, to some extent, to the fact that the Christians, under the instructions of their Emperor, had gathered and brought there literature from all parts of the world, and it was the great seat of learning of the world. On page 128 he refers to a war that was carried on about the great library that had been brought there by the Roman Emperor when he embraced Christianity. Again he says, that when Mohammed locked up the great library be excluded the learned and with them the wealth of the city. In Vol. XIV., page 17, in speaking of the battle of Tanze, he says it was fought over the sacred books that had been deposited there by the ancient Christians. From these indirect references I discovered there must be great deposits of sacred literature in these old libraries. These histories are in the Paris library for the inspection of anyone.

Notwithstanding the art of printing has a tendency to do away with and supersede the written Scriptures, yet there are many valuable manuscripts in existence, some of which are of great value in the interpretation of the Scriptures.

First, the Hebrew manuscripts. These are either rolls designed for the use of synagogues, or square manuscripts, designed for private use. The former are all on parchment and written with the greatest care and accuracy. The others are written on vellum or paper.

Dr. Kennicott says all that are now to be had were written between the tenth and fourteenth centuries. Of course these were written from the originals ; how often they have been rewritten in fourteen hundred years we cannot say, but we know there are many opportunities for change. These manuscripts have been collated by Dr. Kennicott and De Rossi, and amount to 1135 ; but it is more than probable that as the Jewish rabbis did this work they may have left out many things that appeared to them contrary.

The next are the Greek. Of these manuscripts immense numbers still exist. Dr. Holmes has collected 135. Some of these are preserved from the fourth century. Of course, these are not the records that were made when the events they record took place.

Now, reader, our present Bible comes from these manuscripts. The first English Bible was published by J. Wickliffe in 1360, just ninety years before printing was invented. The first Bible printed in our language was by William Tindall, assisted by Miles Coverdale, in 1526. When Tindall was executed for heresy by the Catholics, his works were continued by Coverdale and John Rogers. This book was suppressed time and again, and reprinted by different parties until it went through twenty-two different editions. The last was that which proceeded from the Hampton Court conference in 1603. There were so many errors in the Bishop's Bible that King James's Bible was put on foot and printed in 1611.

Now suppose we consider the many Bibles published by different sects, nations, and individuals, and all coming from these Hebrew, Greek, and Latin manuscripts. The reader must know that the manuscripts have gone through many hands. This we know from the fact that we find Bible manuscripts still in existence, and from these we find Greek manuscripts, Samaritan manuscripts taken from the Hebrew, the Spanish manuscripts, the German manuscripts, the Italian manuscripts, and many others. The reader is referred to the Bodleian Library in the British Museum, and to the libraries at Leyden, Paris, and Rome. We also have some in America, at Philadelphia, in the libraries of the Quakers and in the library of the Antiquarian Society.

The manuscripts of the Hebrew Bible were compiled in the second century. But they never were translated till A.D. 607, by Bishop Adhelm, under the direction of King Alfred. There were a number of parts of these Hebrew manuscripts translated in the second century in the Arabic language. It was printed for the Propaganda at Rome, in 1671, in three volumes. The Armenian version was made in the fourth Century of the Christian era by Miesrob and Isaac, and printed at Amsterdam by Uskin, an Armenian bishop, who was charged by his enemies with following the Vulgate. It was printed at Constantinople in 1705 ; at Venice in 1805. The Coptic New Testament was published by Wilkins at Oxford, 1716.

The Vulgate is an ancient manuscript, taken from the Hebrew and translated into the Latin in the second century ; also one of the Greek and one of the Syriac. These are all of the same date. This Vulgate in the Latin was used in Africa. The Church at Rome was under Greek control at this time and rejected the Latin Vulgate, and used what was called at that time the Vedus Latina, or old Latin. This is the history of Tertullian, Vol. I., page 202.

In the fourth century Jerome tells us there was another translation of the Vulgate, under the instruction of St. Augustine, and St. Jerome recommends this in the highest terms. About the fifth century there was another translation made, which is called the Codex, in the Latin language. There was one at Alexandria, one in the Vatican, and one at Sinai. Parts of these are preserved in the British Museum. They were presented to King Charles by Cyril Lucar, who was patriarch at Constantinople and had been patriarch at Alexandria, and brought these books with him. The Codex of Sinai is in the Greek, and is the same that Dr. Tischendorf found and was declared by the scholars of Leipsic to have been written in the fourth century.

In the year 748 of the Roman Empire and 330 of the Christian era Constantine the Great removed his seat of empire from Rome to Byzantium, and took with him all the records of the Christians to that city, as will be shown in a letter from him in this book in regard to having the Holy Scriptures in manuscript, and having fifty volumes bound and kept on deposit. When Mohammed took possession of Constantinople he had too much respect for these sacred scrolls to let them be destroyed, but had them all nicely cased and deposited in the St. Sophia Mosque. History informs us of the dreadful struggle that took place between the Greeks and Romans over the sacred parchments in the days of the Crusades; and it seems to us that Divine Providence has had something to do with the preservation of these sacred writings. These scrolls look more like rolls of narrow carpet wound round a windlass than anything else. But as I have described them elsewhere I will not attempt a further description here.

Another question arises in the mind of the reader, and that is: How was it possible for these writings to be preserved so long ? I answer that there are many works much older than these in existence. Homer is 900 years older. Why not these? Another reason why these writings have not been brought before the world is that no man has searched for these chronicles as I have done. After getting hold of *Acta Pilati* as I did, accidentally, I made the investigation of these questions my special business for ten years—corresponding with many historians and scholars, sending for all the books that could instruct me on these great questions, engaging two expert scholars, Drs. McIntosh, of Scotland, and Twyman, of England, and going to the city of Rome, paying our way through the Vatican, and then to Constantinople, where we examined those ancient records, sparing neither time nor expense to acquire a knowledge of them. Then it may be asked again: May not I be deceived? May not these men have imposed upon me? To this I would say: That is impossible. Then it might be argued: Might not these writings have been manufactured to make money out of? If so, it was a poor business, for this is the first and only book ever produced from them. It certainly was a bad speculation on their part. But one says: Did not Gregory IX. burn twenty cartloads of these Talmuds? Who says so but a Jewish rabbi? If he did, they were the Talmuds of Babylon, and not those of Jerusalem? There is no body of Christians stronger adherents of Jesus Christ than the Roman Catholics. Why should they want to burn the Talmuds of Jerusalem, which were so full of the doctrines and historical events that are so near and dear to them ? No man can go into the Vatican library without a guard over him, who watches him closely, so that he cannot move a leaf or change a word or letter of anything that is there. If they will not consent to even the slightest change, it is not probable they would burn their works. Men from all over the world are there. Often when we crossed the Tiber, before it was fairly light, there were a thousand strangers between us and St. Peter's gate, waiting to be admitted at the opening of the gate that leads into the Vatican.

One more evidence to the reader : There are at least five hundred quotations made from the Sanhedrim and Talmuds of the Jews by men who have denied their existence. Now I call attention to history, and I will give the name and page, so that all can read for themselves.

First: Rabbi Akiba, a reformed Jewish priest, Vol. I., page 22, quotes from Celsus, an enemy of the Church. He says there was a dreadful earthquake at the time Jesus was crucified, and that the mist that arose from it covered the earth for three hours. On page 28 he says that Jesus was the son of Mary ; that he was the founder of the sect called Christians. On page 48 he says Jesus was crucified on the eve of the Passover. He gives extracts from the apostles, and never denies in a single instance, but admits their genuineness. He quotes the books, and makes extracts from the names they bear. He makes particular mention of his incarnation, of his being born of a virgin, of his being worshipped by the Magi; of his flight into Egypt; of the massacre of the infants of Bethlehem. On page 52 he speaks of his baptism by John and the descent of the Holy Spirit in the form of a dove, and of the voice that was heard out of heaven. He speaks of the miracles done by Jesus, and never doubts the facts in any instance, but attributes them to the art of necromancy he had learned in Egypt. But did the reader ever hear of a thaumaturgist producing a descent of the Holy Spirit or causing voices to be heard from the heavens? Such absurdities are not spoken of except when they are urged against the Christian religion.

Aretas, one of the kings of Arabia, who was a philosopher as well as a king, in speaking of the laws of nature (Vol. VII., page 14), says that Jesus of Judea was a philosopher above the laws of nature; that he controlled all the elements of nature with almighty power; that the winds, thunders, and lightnings obeyed him; and speaks of these facts as being so common that it would be folly to dispute them.

Justin says, in Vol. II., page 42, that the several Roman governors in their respective provinces made reports of the important events that occurred in their jurisdiction, and they were spread on the senatorial dockets at Rome. We find in this same work, page 128, that he appealed to Antoninus and the Senate for clemency for the Christians, and after referring to their many virtues, and to Christ as their leader, added : "And that these things are so, I refer you to the records of the Senate made by Pontius Pilate and others in his day." The learned Tertullian, in his *Apology for Christianity,* about the year 200, after speaking of our Saviour's Crucifixion and Resurrection, and his appearance to the disciples, and ascension into heaven in the sight of the same disciples, who were ordained by him to spread the gospel over the world, thus proceeds: "Of all these things relating to Christ, Pilate himself, in his conscience already a Christian, sent an account to Tiberius, then Emperor." The same writer in the same apology thus relates the proceedings of Tiberius on receiving this information : "There was an ancient decree that no one should be received for a deity unless he was first approved by the Senate. Tiberius, in whose time the Christian name (or religion) had its rise, having received from Palestine, in Syria, an account of such things as confirmed the truth of his (Christ's) divinity, proposed to the Senate that he should be enrolled among the Roman gods, and gave his own prerogative vote in favor of the motion ; but the Senate, without whose consent no deification could take place, rejected it because the Emperor himself had declined the same honor. Nevertheless, the Emperor persisted in his opinion, and threatened punishment to the accusers of the Christians." *Search your own commentaries* (or public writings), *you will there find that Nero was the first who raged with the imperial sword against this sect, then rising most at Rome* (*Horn's Introduction,* Vol. I., page 82).

Now, I would ask, if there were no such records there, would these men have made such appeals? And if they were there, could such things be forged and palmed off on the Roman Senate ? It seems to me to ask the question is enough. Now, if any man will trace out these things he will find that I have as much reason for believing the genuineness of the contents of this book, as I have to believe the genuineness of the Scriptures, looking at the question from a human standpoint. First, you must know that the manuscript from which this book was taken has not gone through so many translations nor been put in so many different languages, from the fact that it is not to be found in another language ; and, secondly, there was no necessity for it, and as to this being forged there was no occasion for that, from the fact it favors no religious denomination, it advocates the tenets of no religious sect. Now I am convinced there was such a man as Herod Antipater, and I know that he could not kill all the male children in a city without giving reasons for it, and there must have been more or less record made of it. I am convinced there was such a man as Herod Antipas, and I know he dare not behead such a man as John the Baptist is represented to be, without a trial, without having to account to some court. I know that Pilate was a Roman officer, and his actions were watched closely and all his public acts had to be recorded upon the Roman dockets.

I do not see why these records should have been destroyed. I am convinced the Jews at that day were looking for a Redeemer, and when the great excitement was reported at Bethlehem it would be not unreasonable that the Jews should make an investigation of the matter; and, again, I know if the Scriptures are true Mary was subject to the death penalty unless she could satisfactorily prove her innocence. I was convinced the Jews must have looked into this matter, and that it would be found recorded somewhere. I knew that if there were such a man as they represented Jesus to be, he could not be tried in the high priest's court and condemned to death, and executed by the Roman authorities, unless there were some record made of it by both the Jews and Romans. Here we have the whole of these records, and why are they not true ? They comport with the Bible; they are just the records we should expect from the Scriptures; they were made or dated at the right time; they came from the place where these records were made; they were written in the same language that was used at that time. Now, if all this is so, why are they not true ?

I offer this book to the public feeling assured it can do no harm to anyone or to any church, but that it will be read by thousands with great interest, and will convince the infidel of the truth of the Scriptures. As Dr. Miller observed: "This book never was needed until now, and it is like all God's providences, always brought out at the right time." Another minister wrote to say he "was more than delighted ;" it was like calling up the dead ; all the circumstances of Calvary were brought vividly before him, and when he read Caiaphas's second report he both wept and rejoiced. Such is the testimony of almost everyone who reads it.

In an extract from a private letter to the *Brunswicker* Dr. Rubin says:

"I saw, while in the Vatican at Rome last week, Dr. W. D. Mahan, of Boonville, Mo., Drs. McIntosh and Twyman, of Scotland, with a number of clerks, both readers; and scribes, going through these old manuscripts and scrolls that have been lying there for hundreds, yea, thousands of years ; they seem to be men of great age and learning, and well qualified for their business. They were going next week to Constantinople to go through the records of the Sanhedrim and the ancient Talmuds of the Jews. Their object is to bring out a new book as a supplement to *Acta Pilati*. I am satisfied, from the character of the men and the nature of the book, it will prove to be one of the most interesting books ever presented to the Christian world, from the fact that all the works on archaeology have been written in such a style that but very few could read and understand them."

CONSTANTINOPLE, TURKEY, October 16, 1883.

TO THE PEOPLE OF NORTH AMERICA.

DEAR FRIENDS: I take pleasure in addressing you this letter, as I feel assured I am doing a good work for my Father who is in heaven. Then, friends, permit me to say to you that I was introduced to my friend, W. D. Mahan, of Boonville, Mo., by my friends of Leipsic, Germany. I engaged to meet him in Paris, France, and when he showed me his plans and the subjects that he wanted, and showed me his notes of reference, the names of others, and books that he had been hunting for ten years, I became satisfied that if we could succeed he would bring out one of the best books ever offered to the Christian world except the Bible. We repaired to the Vatican at Rome, received permission to examine the greatest library in the world, and to my astonishment the first thing we called for was brought to hand in a short time. I mean Pilate's reports, which were more than satisfactory. The next were the Senate's records respecting the investigation of Herod Antipater's conduct at Bethlehem, and Herod Antipas on various charges (one of which was the execution of John the Baptist), the Hillel letters, and the Shammai laws. We then proceeded to Constantinople and went through the records of the Sanhedrim and Talmuds of the Jews that were carried there and preserved by Constantine in the year 337. Here we found Melker's letter (who was priest at Bethlehem at the time that Jesus of Nazareth was born) in respect to the prophecy concerning the birth of Jesus, which is very deep and profound. Next we came upon the report of

Gamaliel, who was sent by the Sanhedrim to interrogate Joseph and Mary concerning the child Jesus, which will prove to be one of the most interesting subjects that was ever read by man. Then the next thing we found was the report of Caiaphas to the Sanhedrim. When read it will awaken the minds of men and give a very different view of this matter to what we have had.

After we had finished the report, Brother Mahan insisted that we should unwind the scroll further, and in doing so we found his second report, which caused us to weep like children, and we both thanked God that we continued the search. We also found many strange historical items, such as will be of great interest to the world at this time. And as Brother Mahan is going to publish his book in America, I can most heartily recommend it.

M. MCINTOSH.

MARKET PLACE, CITY OF ROME, ITALY.

DEAR WIFE: It seems long since I left home, but God is here as well as in America, and it is my chief delight to report you and the children to His throne of mercy daily. I was landed at Marseilles, France, after twelve days out from New York. We had a splendid trip, all but the first two days. We left New York in a gale, and I must confess I was very much alarmed; it seemed to me the water was much higher all around us than where the ship was. That made it more frightful, for it looked as if the ship sunk or was sinking for the first two days. She was sometimes on her end, then on her side, and then would seem to turn almost over; but every tilt she made I prayed

St. Peter's prayer. I think I did more praying the first two days than I had done in two years. But the second day I began to cast up my accounts, not with my Maker, nor with my creditors, but with my stomach. I was awful sick.

Captain Stikes said the storm in starting out made it much worse on us than it would have been if the weather had been clear and calm, but the third day the sea began to calm, and so did my stomach. I was able to go out in the evening, but we were still going up hill; we had no further trouble all the way, but after three or four days it looked as if I would, never get enough to eat. Our fare was poor, much more so than on the English line; so I was told by men that had travelled both lines. I shall return by another route. I met Dr. McIntosh at St. Elgin waiting for me. He is one of the nicest old men and one of the finest scholars I ever met. I feel ashamed in his presence, though he is so grand and noble he can hide my own defects from me better than I can myself. He was very much surprised when I showed him my notes of reference. He did not see how I could get hold of these things so far away. We found Dr. Twyman and his men at the Vatican, and we are working bravely. The very first thing the guard brought was *Acta Palati;* the Doctor was delighted when he saw it. We have two guards; one brings the articles as we call for them; the other sits and watches to see that the books and parchments are not mutilated. To-day was the day of the Pope's holy auditory. We were taken in by the guard, and I must confess I never had such feelings in all my life. The room is, I suppose, three hundred feet or more square; there must have been ten or twelve hundred in the congregation, all men, mostly priests and officers. The Pope is a venerable old man. I saw nothing different in his dress from any other priest; nothing gaudy about him. He sang the mass in the pure old Latin language; his voice was clear and sweet. After he was through quite a number of the priests came and knelt at his feet. He laid his hands gently on each of their heads and pronounced a blessing, but they did not kiss his great toe. I never saw as solemn a congregation in my life ; in fact, it would be impossible for a man to be otherwise in that room. The dome of this room surpasses all the sights my eyes ever beheld; it contains hundreds of windows in the form of eyes with golden lids and lashes, all emitting rays of light of various colors. They seemed so natural I thought I could almost see them wink. They are to represent the all-seeing eye. These eyes are the light of the room. The scene of magnificence beggars description. There are too many things to be described. A man will have a higher appreciation of the Catholic Church, where he sees her enthroned in the hearts of this great church, and I shall ever have a different feeling toward them from what I have had. We have all the text-books we need, Buxtorf, Gesenius, Laportees, and others. We will get through in the Vatican in a few days. We will leave Dr. Twyman and three clerks here, as we find the Hillelite letters and Shemiate and Abtalian laws here in book-form. They will translate such parts of them as we want and send them to me; they will come in a roll. If they come, before I get home, take special care of them. Dr. McIntosh and I, with one clerk, will go to Constantinople, in a day or two. The Doctor has been there, and he thinks he will find all that I want in the St.

Sophia Library. He says the twenty cartloads of Talmuds that history tells us were burned by Gregory IX. were the Talmuds of Babylon, but the Talmuds of Jerusalem are all safe, and so are the records of the Jerusalem Sanhedrim ; that these documents were carried there by Constantine. If so, that is all I want. The Doctor thinks it will be one of the most important books ever brought before the public, except the Bible, as it would give the pros and cons of the outside world at that time. But I have so many things I would like to say and it is now after 1 o'clock A.M. As to home affairs, I am too far off to say anything more, besides I have all confidence in your judgment. I think now that I will be at home by the 10th or 15th of December, and I shall write no more unless something happens. May God bless you; farewell.

W. D. MAHAN.

COLUMBIA, Mo., January 25, 1887.

This is to certify that I am well acquainted with the Rev. W. D. Mahan, of Boonville, Mo. I have known him well for a number of years, having spent several months at his house at different times. I was at his house in Boonville, Mo., shortly after his return (as he then stated to me) from Rome and Constantinople. I gave him some assistance in recopying some of his manuscripts for his book. I saw, examined, and to some extent assisted in arranging the various subjects and chapters in his book.

Judging from the handwriting of said manuscripts, there must have been two or more persons engaged in writing them, as there was a distinct difference in the handwriting. I was impressed at, the time with the belief, from the writing and spelling, that the parties were of foreign birth and education.

I have no interest in this matter, and make the above statement at the request and in justice to the Rev. W. D. Mahan, as an old and valued friend.

J. B. DOUGLASS.

Personally appeared before me, a notary public, within and for the county of Boone, and State of Missouri, General J. B. Douglass, to me well known, and made affidavit to the foregoing certificate.

Witness my hand and notarial seal hereto affixed at Columbia, Mo., this 25th day of January A.D. 1887.

FRANK D. EVANS,
Notary Public.

State of Missouri. County of Cooper, *ss*.

Be it known that on this, the 12th day of January, A.D. 1887, personally came before me, the undersigned, clerk of the Circuit Court of Cooper County, in the State of Missouri, John S. McFarland, well known to me to be a reputable citizen of the city of Boonville, Mo., who, being by me first duly sworn, on his oath says: I have been personally acquainted with Rev. W. D. Mahan for sixteen years or more, and have always found him to be honorable and trustworthy, and a very useful minister in the Church to which he belonged. To my knowledge he was for some time previous to 1883 engaged in preparing himself for a trip to Europe, and that in the fall of 1883 he took leave of his family and friends and started for the cities of Rome and Constantinople to investigate those old records that he said he had found was there on archaeology. After he had been gone some time his wife received a letter from him dated at Rome, Italy. I did not see the postmarks on the letter, but understood it was from Rome.

After some months Mr. Mahan returned and brought quite a lot of manuscripts with him, some of which he read to me, and which were, very interesting. These are as near the facts in the case as I can remember at this time.

JOHN S. McFARLAND.

Subscribed and sworn to before me, on this the 12th day of January, 1887.
Witness my hand and official seal.

CHARLES A. HOUX,
Clerk of Circuit Court of Cooper County. Mo.

By H. A. HUTCHINSON.
State of Missouri, County of Cooper, ss.

Be it known that on this 12th day of January, A.D. 1887, personally came before me, the undersigned, clerk of the Circuit Court of Cooper County, in the State of Missouri, R. W. Whitlow and W. G. Pendleton, composing the firm of Whitlow & Pendleton, real estate and loan agents, of the city of Boonville, in said county, who, being by me first duly sworn, on their oaths say: We have known the Rev. W. D. Mahan, of Boonville, Mo., for a period of more than ten years. He came to our office in the fall of 1883 and told us he was going to Rome with a view to collect materials for a book which he intended to write, and that he had not sufficient money to defray the expenses of the trip ; at his request we loaned him two hundred dollars. Shortly afterward Mr. Mahan disappeared from Boonville, and it was a considerable while before we again met him here at Boonville, when he informed us he had made the trip to Rome, Italy, during the time of his disappearance. A letter purporting to have been written by the said Mahan to his wife from Rome, Italy, was published in a newspaper at Boonville, Mo. Soon after Mr. Mahan reappeared at Boonville he published and circulated his book. Of course we did not follow him to see him at Rome, but the foregoing are the facts within our knowledge.

R. E. WHITLOW,
W. G. PENDLETON,
Attorneys-at-Law.

Subscribed and sworn to before me, on this the 12th day of January, 1887.

CHARLES A. HOUK,
Clerk of Circuit Court, Cooper County, Mo.

CHAPTER II.

A SHORT SKETCH OF THE TALMUDS.

The Hebrew word *lamod* signifies "to teach," and to "teach by example." The word example is always understood. To teach–this is what is meant by tradition. It means that the child learns from its father. From this word we get the word talmud.

We also have the word *shanoh*, which means "to learn," and *gamor*, which means "having learned or having ceased to learn." The Talmuds are written on parchment or papyrus. The scroll is about twenty inches wide, and wound around a roller. From these Talmuds there have been many books written by the Jewish rabbis.

The most important is the *Mishna*. Its name indicates what it is–the Law. It contains the laws of all nations, or a part of the laws of the various nations of the earth, such as the Jewish Sanhedrim thought were compatible with the laws of God. Its principal teachings are what we would call the moral law of God–that is to say, anything is right if God says it is right, and this is the only reason why it is right. This work has been the great reference-book for the Jewish rabbis in all ages. It was translated and compiled by Hillel, and is a very useful book for scholars.

The next in point of value is the *Tosephta*. This word in the Hebrew means "treatment," and contains mainly the ritual of the temple service. It is a very extensive work, and is really a regulator of human life, containing the dealings of husband and wife, parent and child, master and pupil ; in fact, it enters into all the details of life with such thoughtfulness and in such a beautiful style that it should be exceedingly interesting to the young. It certainly contains the finest system of morals in the world.

Then comes the *Mechilta*, which means "government" in the Hebrew language. This book tells of the organization of the Sanhedrim and its powers–both the greater and the less, the greater to be composed of seventy and the less of twenty-four. These two legislative bodies had jurisdiction of the whole of the Jewish commonwealth. Although they possessed great power, it was not absolute. There was another court that exercised the highest authority of the nation. That was the court of elders and priests. This court consisted of twelve men, and its chairman was the high priest. It decided all appeals, and could not be appealed from. This is the court that tried Jesus of Nazareth; and although it was a court of appeals, it had exclusive jurisdiction of capital crimes.

I will give the form of a trial of an accused in this court, as it is given in *Mechilta*. At the time that Jesus was tried by this court the Jewish government had been deprived of its executive power. This was one of the concessions in the capitulation to Augustus Caesar. At this time the Roman Emperor's consent had to be obtained, though he had to use the Jewish soldiers; for the Romans had only one hundred soldiers at Jerusalem. They were continually engaged in war, and needed all their soldiers at home. When an accused person was brought before this court of the high priests, they held a preliminary trial, in order, if possible, to force a plea. If they could not, the accused was sentenced and then sent to the Roman authority, or governor, for his approval. The accused was then remanded to the high priest, and from him to the Sanhedrim, with the charges written out and the names of the witnesses by which they had been proved. If they approved the decision of the high priest, the prisoner was sent back to the high priest for his final trial. This court of twelve men was required by the Jewish law to fast and pray one whole day before the trial commenced; they were then required to bring the Urim and Thummim out of the holy place where they were kept, and to place them before the high priest. The high priest was closely veiled, so that no one could see him, thus representing God doing his work. Then there was what was called the *lactees*, consisting of two men, one of whom stood at the door of the court with a red flag in his hand, and the other sat on a white horse some distance on the road that led to the place of execution. Each of these men continually cried the name of the criminal, his crime, and who were the witnesses, and called upon any person who knew anything in his favor to come forward and testify. After the testimony was taken the eleven men cast lots or voted, and their decision was shown to the high priest. As he was too holy to act by himself, but only as the mouthpiece of God, he went up to a basin or a ewer, as it is called by them, and washed his hands in token of the innocence of the court, thus testifying that the criminal's own action had brought condemnation on himself. As soon as the soldiers saw this, they took the man to the place of execution, and there stoned him till he was dead. Not one of them was allowed to speak, not even to whisper, while the execution was going on. Nothing was heard but the pelting of stones and the shrieks of the criminal. To my mind this would be a most awful mode of death, and one that would be likely to deter others from committing crime.

Now, I ask the reader to consider the mode of a Roman execution, and see what a beautiful chain of divine Providence is brought out in the execution of Jesus of Nazareth. There was a law in the criminal code of the Romans, enacted by Meeleesen, a philosopher by nature, who taught that if a man was accused of a crime and was tried and found not guilty, he should be publicly chastised. His reasons were that the man had acted improperly–so much so that be had created suspicion. This would seem to give license to an enemy to work mischief. But the same philosopher had a remedy at hand, and that was, that any man who accused another and failed to prove it by two witnesses should suffer the punishment the other would have suffered had he been proved guilty. After the whipping was over the Roman officer washed his hands, thereby declaring that the actions of the man had produced his own chastisement. Thus, after Pilate had Jesus scourged he washed his hands, forever clearing the Roman government of the blood of Christ. The reader must remember that the soldiers who brought Jesus from the court of the high priest were Jewish soldiers. They were acquainted with the Jewish custom of washing the hands to condemn. Hence, when they saw Pilate wash his hands they took it for granted that Jesus was to die. One might say that this would relieve the actors of responsibility in this matter. But if a man seeks to injure me, and I by my sagacity avert the injury he intended and change it into a blessing, would that change the guilty intention of the first party?

We also learn from the *Mechilta* that the Jewish commonwealth was divided into districts, such as Palestine, Galilee, Judea, and so on. Each of these states had its courts and legislatures, presided over by a high priest. This is the reason we have so many high priests spoken of in the New Testament history. These states were subdivided into smaller divisions, each of which was presided over by a magistrate who was an officiating priest. If any one will read the *Mechilta,* he will see clearly the government of the United States of North America; and as the laws of the Jewish nation were all dictated by the God of heaven, we should appreciate them the more.

The *Saphra* means, in the Hebrew language, "cornerstone or foundation rock," which goes to show that all these laws were founded upon God's word or authority. This is quite an extended work, and is full of quotations from the various works of the ancient world. I would love to read this carefully for a year and give extracts to the people. I am sure that this little volume will so stir American scholars that these things will be brought before the reading world. But I would advise whoever does it not to trust to the printed copies of the Jewish rabbis, but go as I did to the original manuscript at Byzantium and get it as it was written by its author.

One more book I must call attention to, that is, the *Siphri*. This is more of a chronological and biographical work than anything else, and is by far the most valuable work of them all. It gives the history of the great events of all of them, and mentions the names of all the actors of those events, giving a detailed account of the birth, lineage, deaths, as well as all the wise sayings of such men as Abraham, Joshua, Moses, David, Solomon, and many others. I would like to give many extracts from this work. They would be of deep interest to the American people, as well as of great benefit to the young and rising generation. There is one extract I must give. It will be read with great interest by the Independent Order of Odd Fellows in America:

"Jacob had twelve sons; and when he saw that there were strife and dissatisfaction among them, he went and got him twelve sticks, and when he had bound them together with strong bands, he gave them to his eldest son, and asked him to break them. He tried, but could not. Then he gave them to the next, and so on until each one down to the youngest had tried to break them. And when they had all failed, the father took the bundle of sticks and untied them. He gave one to the eldest and told him to break it. He did so. And then he gave one to the next, and so on, till all the sticks were broken, and each one had done his part. And Jacob said, 'Now, my sons, you must learn two lessons from this: The first lesson is, what neither one of you could do, you all combined can do ; and the second lesson is, when you are all bound together you cannot be broken!'"

Besides these there are the *Pesikta and Midrasham*. These are all full of interesting items, sermons and extracts of sermons, and wise sayings of great men of all ages, the decisions of the great Sanhedrim on points of law and doctrine, and many other questions of great importance, and would be of deep interest to the readers of this day. Now, the reader must bear in mind that these several books that have been noticed are all taken from the Talmud of the Sanhedrim, which was made at Jerusalem. These books were compiled by Hillel the Second, soon after the destruction of the holy city, and were made so that if the scrolls should be destroyed they might be preserved in these. After these, other translations were made to relieve the necessity of the Jews in their dispersed condition, such as the *Nagad, Kikhil, Midrash,* and so on. But, remember, all these works were compiled from the original Talmuds by the Jewish priests, who, of course, would leave out everything that had a tendency to favor the Christian religion. In all such works we need not expect to find anything about Jesus of Nazareth. But this by no means proves that such records are not to be found. We must go to the original scrolls, and there we may expect to get the truth, as the following work will show. Therefore let the reader read and judge for himself.

CHAPTER III.

CONSTANTINE'S LETTER IN REGARD TO HAVING FIFTY COPIES OF THE SCRIPTURES WRITTEN AND BOUND.

It is known that the Roman Emperor, Constantine, who was converted to the Christian religion, had fifty copies of the Scriptures made and placed in the public library for preservation. Some historian has said that they were so large it took two men to open one of them. While in Constantinople I found one of these volumes nicely cased, marked with the Emperor's name and date upon it. To me it was a great curiosity. I got permission with a little *bachsach*, as they call money, to look through it. It was written on *hieotike*, which is the finest of parchment, in large, bold, Latin characters, quite easy to read. As far as I read it had many abbreviations of our present Scriptures, but the facts, sense, and sentences are as full, and, if anything, more complete than our English version. I judge it to be about two and a half by four feet square, and two feet thick. It is well bound, with a gold plate, twelve by sixteen inches, on the front, with a cross and a man hanging on the cross, with the inscription, "Jesus, the Son of God, crucified for the sins of the world." If the Revision Committee had examined and published this work, they might have said they were giving the world something new ; but so far as we examined we saw nothing essentially different from our present Bible. Constantine's letter is on the first page, which we transcribed. The historian will remember that in the *Life of Constantine* (written by Eusebius Pamphili, Bishop of Caesarea, who served him only a few years) Eusebius writes as follows: "Ever mindful of the welfare of those churches of God, the Emperor addressed me personally in a letter on the means of providing copies of the inspired oracles." His letter, which related to providing copies of the Scriptures for reading in the churches, was to the following purport:

"*Victor Constantine Maximus Augustus to Eusebius:* It happens through the favoring of God our Saviour, that great numbers have united themselves to the most holy church in this city, which is called by my name. It seems, therefore, highly requisite, since the city is rapidly advancing in prosperity in all other respects, that the number of churches should also be increased. Do you, therefore, receive with all readiness my determination on this behalf. I have thought it expedient to instruct your Prudence to order fifty copies of the sacred Scriptures, the provisions and use of which you know to be most needful for the instruction of the churches, to be written on prepared parchment, in a legible manner, and in a commodious and portable form, by transcribers thoroughly practised in their art. The procurator of the diocese has also received instructions by letter from our Clemency to be careful to furnish all things necessary for the preparation of such copies, and it will be for you to take special care that they be completed with as little delay as possible. You have authority, also in virtue of this letter, to use two of the public carriages for their conveyance, by which arrangement the copies, when fairly written, will most easily be forwarded for my personal inspection, and one of the deacons of your church may be intrusted with this service, who, on his arrival here, shall experience my liberality. God preserve you, beloved brother."

Now this was done about three hundred and twenty-seven years after the great questions were started, and only about two hundred and seventy years after the last apostle was dead. Suppose some one should write a book denying that such a man as Washington ever lived ; that there never was a revolution of the United States against the King of England ; what would people say of him ? The children of this country would rise up and show him to be false. Then suppose there never was such a man as Jesus Christ; that he never was born at Bethlehem; that he never had any disciples; that they never organized a Christian Church ; and suppose someone should say there was no persecution of the Christian Church for two hundred years; what would you think of a king doing such a thing as making the above-described books ? Remember, too, that nothing was written in those days but the most important affairs of life, because only a few men could write, and the means of writing were limited. Now, the existence of these writings was never denied for twelve to fourteen hundred years afterward. Their intent and spirituality may have been denied, but the facts never were. Now what ought we to think of a man who would deny events that occurred two thousand years ago, that were recorded in the records of kings and historical writers, when he had not one single record to prove it ? How can he know that such records are false? He would have no history, no records of those days to prove it and if they were false, is it not reasonable to think that they would have been proved so then?

CHAPTER IV.

JONATHAN'S INTERVIEW WITH THE BETHLEHEM SHEPHERDS — LETTER OF MELKER, PRIEST OF THE SYNAGOGUE AT BETHLEHEM.

Sanhedrim, 88B. By R. Jose. Order No.2.

JONATHAN, son of Heziel, questions the shepherds and others at Bethlehem in regard to the strange circumstances reported to have occurred there, and reports to this court :

"*Jonathan to the Masters of Israel, Servants of the True God*: In obedience to your order, I met with two men, who said they were shepherds, and were watching their flocks near Bethlehem. They told me that while attending to their sheep, the night being cold and chilly, some of them had made fires to warm themselves, and some of them had laid down and were asleep; that they were awakened by those who were keeping watch with the question, 'What does all this mean? Behold, how light it is!' that when they were aroused it was light as day. But they knew it was not daylight, for it was only the third watch. All at once the air seemed to be filled with human voices, saying, 'Glory ! Glory ! Glory to the most high God !' and, 'Happy art thou, Bethlehem, for God hath fulfilled His promise to the fathers; for in thy chambers is born the King that shall rule in righteousness.' Their shoutings would rise up in the heavens, and then would sink down in mellow strains, and roll along at the foot of the mountains, and die away in the most soft and musical manner they had ever heard; then it would begin again high up in the heavens, in the very vaults of the sky, and descend in sweet and melodious strains, so that they could not refrain from shouting and weeping at the same time. The light would seem to burst forth high up in the heavens, and then descend in softer rays and light up the hills and valleys, making everything more visible than the light of the sun, though it was not so brilliant, but clearer, like the brightest moon. I asked them how they felt–if they were not afraid ; they said at first they were; but after awhile it seemed to calm their spirits, and so fill their hearts with love and tranquillity that they felt more like giving thanks than anything else. They said it was around the whole city, and some of the people were almost scared to death. Some said the world was on fire; some said the gods were coming down to destroy them ; others said a star had fallen; until Melker the priest came out shouting and clapping his hands, seeming to be frantic with joy. The people all came crowding around him, and he told them that it was the sign that God was coming to fulfil His promise made to their father Abraham. He told us that fourteen hundred years before God had appeared to Abraham, and told him to put all Israel under bonds–sacred bonds of obedience; and if they would be faithful, he would give them a Saviour to redeem them from sin, and that he would give them eternal life, and that they should hunger no more; that the time of their suffering should cease forever; and that the sign of his coming would be that light would shine from on high, and the angels would announce his coming, and their voices should be heard in the city, and the people should rejoice: and a virgin that was pure should travail in pain and bring forth her first born, and he should rule all flesh by sanctifying it and making it obedient. After Melker had addressed the people in a loud voice, he and all the old Jews went into the synagogue and remained there praising God and giving thanks.

"I went to see Melker, who related to me much the same as the shepherds had reported. He told me that he had lived in India, and that his father had been priest at Antioch; that he had studied the sacred scrolls of God all his life, and that he knew that the time had come, from signs given, for God to visit and save the Jews from Roman oppression and from their sins; and as evidence he showed me many quotations on the tripod respecting the matter.

"He said that next day three strangers from a great distance called on him, and they went in search of this young child; and they found him and his mother in the mouth of the cave, where there was a shed projecting out for the sheltering of sheep ; that his mother was married to a man named Joseph, and she related to them the history of her child, saying that an angel had visited her, and told her that she should have a son, and she should call him Jesus, for he should redeem his people from their sins; and he should call her blessed forever more.

"Whether this is true or not remains to be proved in the future. There have been so many impostors in the world, so many babes born under pretended miracles, and all have proved to be a failure, that this one may be false, this woman only wishing to hide her shame or court the favor of the Jews.

"I am informed that she will be tried by our law, and,

if she can give no better evidence of her virtue than she has given to Melker, she will be stoned according to our law, although, as Melker says, there never has been a case before with such apparent divine manifestations as were seen on this occasion. In the past, in various instances, virgins have pretended to be with child by the Holy Ghost, but at the time of their delivery there was no light from the heavens, and no angels talking among the clouds and declaring that this was the King of the Jews. And, as to the truth of these things, the whole of the people of Bethlehem testify to having seen it, and the Roman guard also came out and asked what it meant, and they showed by their actions that they were very much alarmed. These things, Melker says, are all declared in the Scriptures to be the sign of His coming. Melker is a man of great learning and well versed in the prophecies, and he sends you this letter, referring you to those prophecies :

" '*Melker, Priest of the Synagogue of Bethlehem, to the Higher Sanhedrim of the Jews at Jerusalem:*

" 'HOLY MASTERS OF ISRAEL: I, your servant, would call your attention to the words of the prophet in regard to the forerunner, and the rise as well as the conductor of a great and mighty nation, wherein should dwell the true principles of righteousness and the conductor of the outward formation of a national domain of God upon earth. As evidence of the fact, the vision and affliction that has befallen Zacharias of late is enough to satisfy all men of the coming of some great event; and this babe of Elizabeth is the beginning of better times.

"'What has occurred here in the last few days, as Jonathan will inform you, forever settles the question that the day of our redemption is drawing nigh. The sections of these divisions are three: First, the general survey; the original foundation and destiny of man in his single state; the proto-evangel ; the full development of mankind; the promises to the fathers of the covenant people; Judah, the leader tribe; section second, the Mosaic law and the Mosaic outlook ; the prophecy of Baalam; section third, the anointed one; and the prophets of the past exile: Haggai, Zechariah, and Malachi ; Malachi's prophecy of the forerunner of the Lord. Now, noble masters of Israel, if you will refer to the several sections of the divine word, you will not fail to see that all that has been spoken by the prophets in regard to the works of God upon earth has been fulfilled in the last few days in the two events, the birth of the child of Elizabeth and that of Mary of Bethlehem.

"'The unlimited freedom which some men take with these holy writings of God, as to the above prophecy, subjects us to the severest criticism. It is, however, most satisfactory to see and hear that the divine grandeur and authority of the sacred oracles are in no way dependent on the solution of carnal critics, but rest on an inward light shining everywhere out of the bosom of a profound organic unity and an interconnected relation with a consistent and united teleology ; overleaping all time, the historical present as well as the past, and all the past brought to light in these two events that have just transpired. Indeed, all past time is blending with the present horizon, and the works of God in ages past are just beginning to develop themselves at this particular time, and the present scenes are bringing us close on to the ways of God upon earth. While we reverence these men of God, we should not misquote their language. Take, for example, the third section of Isaiah, where he prophesies of the captive Israelites, instead of his consolation to the captive. While one of his words refers to the future condition and the reason therefor, the other is sweet in consolation of the Israelites while in this state of captivity, and full of the blessed promises in the future.

" 'But let the spirit of prophecy bear us on with the prophet into future time, far beyond the kingdoms of this world into a glorious future, regardless of the Roman, Babylonian, or even the Maccabeean rule or rulers; but never forgetting that the prophet is one who is divinely inspired, and is called, commissioned, and qualified to declare the will as well as the knowledge of God. Yes, he is a seer. His prophecy is of the nature of a vision, involving and enveloping all the faculties of the soul, and placing the prophet in the attitude to God of being outside the body and independent of it. Yet, far better without the body than with it; for the further the soul gets from the body the more active it becomes. This fact is demonstrated in our dreams. The vivid powers of the soul are much more active in dreams than at any other time, the perception is clearer, and the sensitive faculties are much more alive when asleep than when awake. We see this verified in the man dying. His eye is usually brighter, his mind is clearer, his soul is freer and less selfish, as be passes on and nears the eternal state.

" 'So is the prophet. He becomes so personal with God that he uses the personalities with seeming presumption; while it is the indwelling power of God's spirit inflating the soul and setting the tongue on fire. So was the moving language of the words to which you have been referred. It seems to me those men of God saw distinctly the gathering light; they saw the travailing of the virgin, they saw the helpless infant in the sheep trough ; they heard the mighty chanting of the heavenly host; they saw the ambition of human nature in the Roman soldiery aiming to destroy the child's life; and in that infant they saw human nature in its fallen and helpless condition ; and it appears as if they saw the advance of that infant into perfect manhood. As he becomes the theme of the world, his advancing nature will triumph over all; as he does escape the Roman authority this day, so he will finally triumph over all the world, and even death itself shall be destroyed.

" 'We, as Jews, place too much confidence in the outward appearance, while the idea we get of the kingdom of heaven is all of a carnal nature, consisting of forms and ceremonies. The prophecies referred to, and many other passages that I might mention, all go to show that the kingdom of God is to begin within us, in the inner life, and rule there, and from the inner nature all outward actions are to flow in conformity with the revealed and written teachings and commands of God. So is the spirit of prophecy. While it uses the natural organs of speech, it at the same time controls all the faculties of life, producing sometimes a real ecstacy, not mechanical or loss of consciousness, though cut off for the time from external relations. He is thus circumscribed to speak, as did Balaam, the words of God with human life. This is to be held by us Jews as of the first and greatest importance, and we are to remember that his prophecy has the same reference to the future that it does to the past, and has respect to the whole empire of man. While it specifies individuals and nations, it often has reference to doctrines and principles ; and in this light Israel is the result of prophecy, as a nation with her religious teachings. So is this virgin's babe born to be a ruler of all nations of the earth. The Torah itself goes back to prophecy, as well as every prophet stands on the Torah, and on this rests all prophecy pronouncing condemnation on the disobedient and blessings on the faithful. It was on this principle that the covenant of inheritance was made with Abraham, and, in reality, so made with David. Thus all the promises, political, ethical, judicial, and ritual, rest on the Torah. In short, the whole administration finds its authority in the prophetic vision, as set forth by the commands of God, to regulate human life commencing in the inner life and working outward, until the outward is like the inward ; and thus advancing on from individuals to nations.

" 'The Messianic prophecy has no other justification than this. On this rests the church, and on this rests the theocracy. On this rests the glory of the future kingdom of God upon earth.

" 'The whole chain of prophecy is already fulfilled in this babe; but the development is only commencing. He will abolish the old cultus forever, but with man it will develop commensurate with time itself. There are many types in the shadow, in the plant, in the animal. Every time the Romans celebrated a triumph on the Tiber it shadowed forth the coming Caesar ; so every suffering of David, or lamentation of Job, or glory of Solomon–yea, every wail of human sorrow, every throe of human grief, every dying sigh, every falling bitter tear—was a type, a prophecy of the coming King of the Jews and the Saviour of the world. Israel stands as a common factor at every great epoch of history. The shading of the colors of the prophetic painting does not obliterate the prediction of the literal Israel's more glorious future in the kingdom of God. Her historic calling to meditate salvation to the nations is not ended with this new-comer on the stage of earthly life. The prophecy is eschatological, refining the inner life as well as shaping the outer life in conformity to good laws. Looking also to the end of time and its great importance to us, it has something to teach, and we have something to learn. Along the ages past all the great, good, and happy have first learned their duties, and then performed them: and thus for thousands of years Israel has stood, hope never dying in the Hebrew heart, and has been the only appointed source of preserved knowledge of the true God. And this day she stands as the great factor and centre around which all nations of the earth must come for instruction to guide them, that they may become better and happier.

" 'These sacred scrolls which we Jews received from God by the hand of Moses are the only hope of the world. If they were lost to mankind, it would be worse than putting out the sun, moon, and all the stars of night, for this would be a loss of sacred light to the souls of men. When we consider the surroundings, there never has been a time more propitious than the present for the establishing of the true religion, and it seems, by reviewing our history for hundreds of years past, that this is. the time for the ushering in of the true kingdom of God. The nations of the earth that have been given to idolatry are growing tired of placing confidence in and depending on gods that do not help them in the hour of danger, and they are now wanting a God that can and will answer their calls.

"'King Herod sent for me the other day, and after I related to him of the God of the Jews and His works, of the many and mighty deeds He had performed for our fathers and for us as a nation, he seemed to think, if there was such a God as we professed, it was far better than to depend on such gods as the Romans had made, of timber, stone, and iron; and even the gods of gold were powerless. He said that if he could know that this babe that was declared by the angels, was such a God as he that saved the Israelites in the Red Sea, and saved Daniel, and those three from the fearful heat of fire, he would have pursued quite a different course toward him. He was under the impression that he had come to drive the Romans from their possessions, and to reign as a monarch instead of Caesar. And I find this to be the general feeling throughout the world, so far as I can hear; that the people want and are ready to receive a God that can demonstrate in his life that he is such a God that the race of men can depend on in time of trouble ; and if he can show such power to his friends he will be feared by his enemies, and thus become universally obeyed by all nations of the earth. And this, I fear, is going to be a trouble with our nation ; our people are going to look to him as a temporal deliverer, and will aim to circumscribe him to the Jews alone; and when his actions begin to flow out to all the inhabitants of the world in love and charity, as is most certainly shown forth in the ninth section of the holy prophet, then I fear the Jews will reject him ;

and, in fact, we are warned of that already in the third section of Jeremiah's word. To avoid this Israel must be taught that the prophecy of Isaiah does not stop with the Babylonian captivity and return to the kingdom of heaven, and that Ezekiel's wheels do not whirl politically or spiritually in heaven, but upon earth, and have reference to earthly revolutions or changes, and show the bringing to pass of the great events of which this of Bethlehem is the grandest of all.

" 'Neither is the outlook of Daniel to be confined to the shade of the Maccabeean wall of Jewish conquest. Nor are these great questions to be decided by our unsuccessful attempts to find out what the prophet meant or what he might have understood himself to mean; but from the unity, totality, and organic connection of the whole body of prophecy, as referring to the kingdom of this world becoming subject to the kingdom of the Saviour of all men. We, as Jews, are the only people that God has intrusted with the great questions, and, of course, the world will look to and expect us to give interpretation to these questions ; and as we are intrusted with these things, God will hold us responsible if we fail to give the true light on this subject. Up to this time I am fearful the Jews as a nation are as much divided, and perhaps as much mistaken, as to the nature of His works, as any other people. I find, by conversing with the Romans, Greeks, and others, that all their knowledge of these things of Jewish expectation of a Redeemer has been obtained from the Jews, either directly or indirectly, and it was through them Herod got the idea of his being a temporal King, and to rule and reign by the might of carnal weapons; whereas, if we consult the spiritual import of the prophets, his office is to blend all nations in one common brotherhood. and establish love in the place of law, and that heart should throb high with love to heart, and under this law a universal peace. Wherever one should meet another they should meet as friends; for what else can the prophet mean, in section nine, where he shows that this King shall destroy all carnal weapons and convert them to a helpful purpose, and thus become the active worker in doing good to all men, and teaching all men to do good to each other?

" 'By reading all the scrolls of God we find that the unity and totality of all the prophets go to bear us out in this idea, and all have reference to this Babe of Bethlehem. If we consult them as to the time, taking the revolutions of Ezekiel's wheels, they show plainly that the revolutions of the different governments of the world fix this as the time. Next, consult them in regard to the individuals connected with this great event. These are pointed to as the virgin wife, by Zacharias; next, the place has been pointed out and named ; then the light and the appearing of the angels have all been set forth, and also the opposition of the Romans has been declared. Now, I ask the High Court of the living God to look well on these things, and tell us how men that lived in different ages of the world, that lived in different portions of the country–men that never knew each other–men that were not prophesying for a party–men that had no personal interest in the subject as men–men that jeopardized, and some of them lost their lives on account of having uttered these prophecies–how could they all point out the place, the time, and the names of the parties so plain and clear, if it was not revealed to them and ordained by God himself? I understand that the Romans and some of the priests have been saying that Zacharias was a hypocrite, and that Mary was a bad woman. Such might be the case, so far as man is able to judge; but who, I ask, can forge such truth as these prophecies, and make them come true? Or who can cause light to descend from the heavens and the angels come down and make the declaration that this was the Son of God, King of the Jews?

" 'Noble Masters of the Sanhedrim, I was not alone. I am not the only witness of these things. The principal people of Bethlehem saw them and heard them as I did. I would say to you, if this is not the Jews' King, then we need not look for any other; for every line of prophecy has been most completely fulfilled in him; and if he does not appear and save his own people I shall despair of ever being released, and I shall believe that we have misinterpreted the meaning of all the prophets. But I feel so sure that this is he I shall wait in expectation and with much anxiety, and I have no fears of any harm befalling him. All the Romans in the world cannot harm him; and although Herod may rage, may destroy all the infants in the world, the same angels that attended his birth will watch over him through life, and the Romans will have to contend with the same God that Pharaoh did, and will meet with similar defeat.'"

CHAPTER V.

GAMALIEL'S INTERVIEW WITH JOSEPH AND MARY AND OTHERS CONCERNING JESUS.

The *hagiographa* or holy writings, found in the St. Sophia mosque at Constantinople, made by Gamaliel, in the Talmuds of the Jews, 27 B. It seems Gamaliel was sent by the Sanhedrim to interrogate Joseph and Mary in regard to this child Jesus. He *says :*

"I found Joseph and Mary in the city of Mecca, in the land of Ammon or Moab. But I did not find Jesus. When I went to the place where I was told he was, he was somewhere else ; and thus I followed him from place to place, until I despaired of finding him at all. Whether he knew that I was in search of him and did it to elude me, I cannot tell, though I think it most likely the former was the reason, for his mother says he is bashful and shuns company.

"Joseph is a wood-workman. He is very tall and ugly. His hair looks as though it might have been dark auburn when young. His eyes are gray and vicious. He is anything but prepossessing in his appearance, and he is as gross and glum as he looks.

He is but a poor talker, and it seems that yes and no are the depth of his mind. I am satisfied he is very disagreeable to his family. His children look very much like him, and upon the whole I should call them a third-rate family. I asked him who were his parents. He said his father's name was Jacob, and his grandfather was

Matthew. He did not like to talk on the subject. He is very jealous. I told him that we had heard that he had had a vision, and I was sent to ascertain the facts in the case. He said he did not call it a vision; he called it a dream. He said after he and Mary had agreed to marry, it seemed that something told him that Mary was with child ; that he did not know whether he was asleep or awake, but it made such an impression on his mind that he concluded to have nothing more to do with her; and while he was working one day under a shed, all at once a man in snowy white stood by his side, and told him not to doubt the virtue of Mary, for she was holy before the Lord ; that the child conceived in her was not by man, but by the Holy Ghost, and that the child would be free from human passions. In order to do this he must–that is, his humanity must–be of the extract of *almah* (that is the Hebrew word for virgin), that he might endure all things, and not resist, and fill the demands of prophecy. He said the angel told him that this child should be great and should rule all the kingdoms of this world. He said that this child should set up a new kingdom, wherein should dwell righteousness and peace, and that the kingdoms of this world which should oppose him God would utterly destroy. I asked him, How could a virgin conceive of herself without the germination of the male? He said : "This is the work of God. He has brought to life the womb of Elizabeth, so she had conceived and will bear a son in her old age who will go before and tell the people of the coming of this King." After telling me all these things, he disappeared like the melting down of a light. I then went and told Mary what had occurred, and she told me that the same angel, or one like him, had appeared to her and told the same things. So I married Mary, thinking that if what the angel had told us was true, it would be greatly to our advantage ; but I am fearful we are mistaken. Jesus seems to take no interest in us, nor anything else much. I call him lazy and careless. I do not think he will ever amount to much, much less be a king. If he does, he must do a great deal better than he has been doing.' I asked him how long after that interview with the angel before the child was born. He said he did not know, but he thought it was seven or eight months. I asked him where they were at the time. He said in Bethlehem. The Roman commander had given orders for all the Jews to go on a certain day to be enrolled as taxpayers, and he and Mary went to Bethlehem as the nearest place of enrollment; and while there this babe was born. I asked if anything strange occurred there that night. He said that the people were much excited, but he was so tired that he had gone to sleep, and saw nothing. He said toward day there were several priests came in to see them and the babe, and gave them many presents. And the news got circulated that this child was to be King of the Jews, and it created such an excitement that he took the child and his mother and came to Moab for protection, for fear the Romans would kill the child to keep it from being a rival to the Romans.

"I discovered that all Joseph's ideas were of a selfish kind. All he thought of was himself. Mary is altogether a different character, and she is too noble to be the wife of such a man. She seems to be about forty or forty-five years of age, abounds with a cheerful and happy spirit and is full of happy fancies. She is fair to see, rather fleshy, has soft and innocent-looking eyes, and seems to be naturally a good woman. I asked her who her parents were, and she said her father's name was Eli, and her mother's name was Anna; her grandmother's name was Pennel, a widow of the tribe of Asher, of great renown. I asked her if Jesus was the son of Joseph. She said he was not. I asked her to relate the circumstances of the child's history. She said that one day while she was grinding some meal there appeared at the door a stranger in shining raiment, which showed as bright as the light. She was very much alarmed at his presence, and trembled like a leaf; but all her fears were calmed when he spoke to her; for he said: 'Mary, thou art loved by the Lord and He has sent me to tell thee that thou shalt have a child; that this child shall be great and rule all nations of the earth.' She continued : 'I immediately thought of my engagement to Joseph, and supposed that was the way the child was to come; but he astonished me the more when he told me that cousin Elisabeth had conceived and would bear a son, whose name was to be John; and my son should be called Jesus. This caused me to remember that Zacharias had seen a vision and disputed with the angel, and for that he was struck with dumbness, so that he could no longer hold the priest's office. I asked the messenger if Joseph knew anything of the matter. He said that he told Joseph that I was to have a child by command of the Holy Ghost, and that he was to redeem his people from their sins, and was to reign over the whole world; that every man should confess to him and he should rule over all the kings of the earth.'

"I asked her how she knew that he was an angel, and she said he told her so, and then she knew he was an angel from the way he came and went. I asked her to describe how he went away from her, and she said that he seemed to melt away like the extinguishing of a light. I asked her if she knew anything of John the Baptist. She said he lived in the mountains of Judea the last she knew of him. I asked her if he and Jesus were acquainted, or did they visit. She said she did not think they knew each other.

"I asked her if at the time this angel, as she called him, visited her, she was *almah* (that is, virgin). She said she was; that she had never showed to man, nor was known by any man. I asked her if she at that time maintained her *fourchette;* and after making her and Joseph understand what I meant, they both said she had, and Joseph said this was the way he had of testing her virtue. I asked her if she knew when conception took place. She said she did not. I asked her if she was in any pain in bearing, or in delivering this child. She said, 'None of any consequence.' I asked her if he was healthy; to give me a description of his life. She said he was perfectly healthy; that she never heard him complain of any pain or dissatisfaction ; his food always agreed with him; that he would eat anything set before him, and if anyone else complained, he would often say he thought it good enough, much better than we deserved. She said that Joseph was a little hard to please, but this boy had answered him so often, and his answers were so mild and yet so suitable, that he had almost broken him of finding fault. She said he settled all the disputes of the family; that no odds what was the subject or who it was, one word from him closed all mouths, and what gave him such power was his words were always unpretending and spoken as though they were not intended as a rebuke, but merely as a decision. I asked her if she had ever seen him angry or out of humor. She said she had seen him apparently vexed and grieved at the disputes and follies of others, but had never seen him angry. I asked her if he had any worldly aspirations after money or wealth, or a great name, or did he delight in fine dress, like the most of youth. She said that was one thing that vexed her, he seemed to take no care of his person ; he did not care whether he was dressed or not, or whether the family got along well or ill; it was all alike to him. She said she talked to him about it, and he would look at her a little grieved and say, 'Woman (for such he always called me), you do not know who I am.' Indeed, she said he takes so little interest in the things of the world and the great questions of the day, they were beginning to despair of his ever amounting to much-much less be a king, as the angel said he would be; if so, he would have to act very differently from what he was acting at that time. I told her that the Jewish doctors contended that the amorous disposition is peculiar to the male. I asked her if she had ever seen in the private life of Jesus any signs of such disposition. She said she had not. I asked if she saw in him any particular fondness for female society. She said she had not ; if anything, rather the contrary ; that the young *bethaul* (the word in the Hebrew for young women) were all very fond of him, and were always seeking his society, and yet he seemed to care nothing for them; and if they appeared too fond of him, he treated them almost with scorn. He will often get up and leave them, and wander away and spend his time in meditation and prayer. He is a perfect ascetic in his life. 'When I see how the people like to be with him, and ask him questions, and seem to take such delight with his answers–both men and women–it almost vexes me. They say there is a young woman in Bethany whom he intends to marry ; but unless he changes his course very much he will never be qualified to have a family. But I do not believe the report. He never seems to me to care anything about women when he is in my presence.'

"Thus it seems that Joseph and Mary have both lost all confidence in his becoming anything. They seem to think that the Sanhedrim should do something for him to get him out and let him show himself to the people. I tried to console them by telling them that my understanding of the prophecy was that he had to come to the high priesthood first, and there work in the spiritual dominion of the heart; and when he had brought about a unity of heart and oneness of aim, it would be easy enough to establish his political claim; and all who would not willingly submit to him, it would be an easy matter with the sword of Joshua or Gideon to bring under his control. It seemed to me that his parents' ideas are of a selfish character; that they care nothing about the Jewish government nor the Roman oppression. All they think of is self-exaltation, and to be personally benefited by their son's greatness. But I told them they were mistaken ; that the building up of the kingdom of heaven was not to be done by might nor by power, but by the Spirit of the Lord, and it would not do for us to use carnal weapons, nor to expect carnal pleasures to be derived therefrom; that it was not my understanding of the prophecy that this king was to use such weapons either for himself or for the benefit of a party, but for the good of all men; that his dominion was to be universal, and it was to be of a spiritual character ; that he was sent to the lost and not to the found.

"His parents told me of an old man who lived on the road to Bethany who had once been a priest, a man of great learning, and well skilled in the laws and prophets, and that Jesus was often there with him reading the law and prophets together; that his name was Massalian, and that I might find Jesus there. But he was not there. Massalian said he was often at Bethany with a young family, and he thought there was some love affair between him and one of the girls. I asked him if he had seen anything like a courtship between them. He said he had not, but inferred from their intimacy and from the fondness on the woman's part, as well as from the laws of nature, that such would be the case. I asked him to give me an outline of the character of Jesus. He said that he was a young man of the finest thought and feeling he ever saw in his life ; that he was the most apt in his answers and solutions of difficult problems of any man of his age he had ever seen ; that his answers seem to give more universal satisfaction-so much so that the oldest philosopher would not dispute with him, or in any manner join issue with him, or ask the second time. I asked Massalian who taught him to read and interpret the law and the prophets. He said that his mother said that he had always known how to read the law; that his mind seemed to master it from the beginning; and into the laws of nature and the relation of man to his fellow in his teachings or talks, he gives a deeper insight, inspiring mutual love and strengthening the common trust of society. Another plan he has of setting men right with the laws of nature : he turns nature into a great law book of illustrations, showing that every bush is a flame, every rock a fountain of water, every star a pillar of fire, and every cloud the one that leads to God. He makes all nature preach the doctrine of trust in the divine Fatherhood. He speaks of the lilies as pledges of God's care, and points to the fowls as evidence of his watchfulness over human affairs. Who can measure the distance between God and the flower of the field ? What connection is there between man and the lily? By such illustrations he creates a solicitude in man that seems to awe him into reverence, and he becomes attracted toward heavenly thought, and feels that he is in the presence of one that is superior. In this talk he brings one to feel he is very near the presence of God. He says how much more your Father. The plane is one, though the intermediate points are immeasurably distant. Thus by beginning with a flower he reasons upward to the absolute, and then descends and teaches lessons of trust in a loving Father. The lessons of trust in God reassure the anxious listener and create an appetite that makes him long for more; and it often seems, when he has brought his hearers to the highest point of anxiety, he suddenly breaks out and leaves his company as though he cared nothing for them. Jesus in his talk brings all these illustrations to make man feel his nearness to his kindred, man, teaching also their relation to and dependence upon God; and although his method is happy, it does not seem to me that it is the most successful. He teaches that man and the flowers and birds drink from the same fountain and are fed from the same table, yet at the same time he seems to do everything to excite suspicion and prejudice. We that are watching him to see his divine mission commence, he is continually tantalizing our expectations, as well as mocking our natural reason and desires. When a man separates himself from all other men, both in point of doctrine as well as discipline, he takes a very great risk on his part-especially when he confines God to one channel, and that one of his own dictation. A man that assumes these responsible positions must have vast resources from which to draw, or he will sink in the whirlpool which his own impertinence has created. Through Jesus, in his teachings or talks (his words sound so much like the teachings of Hillel or Shammai that I must call it teaching, though he has no special scholars), we learn that God is Spirit, and God is Father; and he says these are the only two things that are essential for man to know. Then he illustrates this to the parents, and asks them what would they do for their children. He was telling some mothers a circumstance of a mother starving herself to feed her child, and then applied it to God as our Father; and they commenced shouting, they were so happy; and Jesus got up and left the house in seeming disgust.

"Massalian says he is tempted at times to become

impatient with Jesus, as he devotes so much time to details. It seems almost a waste of time for a man who came to save the world to be lingering over a special case of disease. He thinks he could hasten Jesus's physical deportment. Why not speak one word and remove every sick patient from his sick-bed at the same hour? What a triumph this would be. I asked him if Jesus had healed anyone. He said not as yet; but if he is to be King of the Jews, he was to heal all nations, and why not do it at once? If he would, there would be nothing more required to establish his kingship. But I said to him, 'Is it not equally so with God's creative power? See what time and labor it takes to bring forth a grain of corn. Why not have caused the earth to bring forth every month instead of every year? Christ was talking in defence of his Father. The people must learn to love and obey the Father before they would reverence the Son. Yes, he said the God that Jesus represented was one that the people might love and venerate; that he was a God of love, and had no bloody designs to execute on even a bad man, provided he ceased his evil ways.'

"It is to be noted that in all Jesus's talk there are manifest references to the future. Many of his statements were like a sealed letter–not to be opened but by time. A grain of mustard was to result in a large tree. All his ideas refer to the future; like the parent helping the child with his burden of to-day, by telling of the blessings of tomorrow; and by making to-day the seed-corn of tomorrow; keeping the action of to-day under moral control by making the morrow the day of judgment. He stated further that Jesus was a young man who was the best judge of human nature he had ever seen ; that he thought at times he could tell men their thoughts and expose their bad principles; and while he had all these advantages of life, he seemed not to care for them nor to use them abusively. He seems to like all men—one as well as another—so much so that his own parents have become disgusted with him, and have almost cast him off. But Jesus has such a peculiar temperament that he seems not to care, and is as well satisfied with one as another. He said that Jesus seemed fond of Mary and Martha, who lived at Bethany, and probably I might find him there.

Massalian is a man of very deep thought and most profound judgment. All his life he has made the Scriptures his study. He, too, is a good judge of human nature, and he is satisfied that Jesus is the Christ. He said that Jesus seemed to understand the prophecy by intuition. I asked him where Jesus was taught to read the prophecy. He said that his mother told him that Jesus could read from the beginning ; that no one had ever taught him to read. He said that he, in making quotations from the prophets, was sometimes mistaken or his memory failed him ; but Jesus could correct him every time without the scroll ; and that sometimes he thought Jesus was certainly mistaken, but never in a single instance was he wrong. I asked him to describe his person to me, so that I might know him if I should meet him. He said: 'If you ever meet him you will know him. While he is nothing but a man, there is something about him that distinguishes him from every other man. He is the picture of his mother, only he has not her smooth, round face. His hair is a little more golden than hers, though it is as much from sunburn as anything else. He is tall, and his shoulders are a little drooped ; his visage is thin and of a swarthy complexion, though this is from exposure. His eyes are large and a soft blue, and rather dull and heavy. The lashes are long, and his eyebrows very large. His nose is that of a Jew. In fact, he reminds me of an old-fashioned Jew in every sense of the word. He is not a great talker, unless there is something brought up about heaven and divine things, when his tongue moves glibly and his eyes light up with a peculiar brilliancy; though there is this peculiarity about Jesus, he never argues a question ; he never disputes. He will commence and state facts, and they are on such a solid basis that nobody will have the boldness to dispute with him. Though he has such mastership of judgment, he takes no pride in confuting his opponents, but always seems to be sorry for them. I have seen him attacked by the scribes and doctors of the law, and they seemed like little children learning their lessons under a master. His strongest points are in the spiritual power of the law and the intentions of the prophets. The young people tried to get him to take a class of them and teach them ; but he utterly refused.' This Jew is convinced that he is the Messiah of the world.

"I went from there to Bethany, but Jesus was not there. They said he and Lazarus were away, they could not tell where. I went and saw Mary and Martha, the sisters of Lazarus, and had a long talk with them. They are very pleasant and nice young maids, and Mary is quite handsome. I teased her about Jesus, but they both denied that Jesus was anything like a lover; he was only a friend–though this is so common for young maids I did not know whether to believe them or not until I told them my real business. And when I told them that this was the same person that was born of the virgin in Bethlehem some twenty-six years before, and that his mother had told me all the facts in the case, they seemed deeply interested. They then told me upon their honor that Jesus never talked or even hinted to either one of them on the subject of marriage. Martha blushed, and said she wished he had. If he was to be a king, she would like to be queen. I asked them if they had ever seen him in the company of young virgins. They said they had not. I asked them if they had heard him talk about young girls, or if he sought their society more than that of men ; and they both declared they had not; and they were very much surprised that he did not. I asked them what he talked of when in their company; and they said he was not much in their company; that he and their brother would go upon the housetop and stay there half the night, and sometimes all night, talking and arguing points of interest to them both. Mary said she had often gone near, so she could listen to them, for she loved to hear him talk, he was so mild and unpretending, and then was so intelligent that he was different from any and all other young men she had ever seen. I asked them what was their brother's opinion of him. They said he thought there never was such a man on earth. He thought him to be one of God's prophets. He said when they are out in the mountains, as they are most all the time, Jesus can tell him all about the flowers, trees, and rocks, can tell him everything in the world, and that none of the wild animals are afraid of him. He says often the stag and the wolf will come and stand for Jesus to stroke their mane, and seem almost loath to go away from him. He says that no poisonous serpent will offer to hiss at him. Their brother thinks he is perfectly safe if Jesus is with him. I asked them if he had ever told their brother anything about himself. They said that if he had spoken to their brother he had not told them.

"Now, Masters of Israel, after having investigated this matter ; after tracing Jesus from his conception to the present time ; after obtaining all the information that is to be had on this important subject, getting it from those who are more likely to tell the truth from the fact they are disinterested persons; and then taking a prophetical as well as a historical view of the subject, I have come to the conclusion that this is the Christ that we are looking for. And as a reason for my conclusion, I will call your attention to the following facts : First to the prophecy of Isaiah, section 7 : 'And he said, Hear now, saith the Lord. Oh, house of David, is it a small thing for you ? Therefore the Lord himself shall give you a sign ; behold, a virgin shall conceive and bear a son, and shall call his name God with men. Butter and honey shall he eat, that he may know to refuse the evil and choose the good; for before the child shall know to refuse the evil and choose the good the land that God abhorrest shall be forsaken of her king.' Section 8 : 'Bind the testimony ; seal the law among his disciples; the Lord will hide his face from the house of Jacob, and he will look for him.' Here is a literal fulfillment of this word of the Most High God, so clear and plain that none may mistake. Jeremiah, 31st section : 'Turn, oh virgin, to thy people, for the hand of the Lord is upon thee; for the Lord shall create a new thing in the earth; a woman shall compass a man.' Here again are set forth the same things that Isaiah speaks of, and the same things that I have learned from Mary. Micah, section 5: 'Thou, Bethlehem Ephratah, thou art little among the thousands of Judah out of thee shall come forth unto me him that shall rule my people. He is from everlasting; and I will give them up until the time she travaileth to bring forth my first born, that he may rule all people.' Here we have the city, the virgin, the office, his manner of life, the seeking him by the Sanhedrim. All these things are under our eyes as full and complete as I now write them, who have all this testimony given in this letter. How can we as a people dispute these things? In the 49th section of Genesis, making reference to the history, that is now upon us, the writer says: 'A captive shall not depart from Judah, nor a lawmaker from him, until Shiloh come, and gather his people between his feet, and keep them forever.' "

CHAPTER VI.

REPORT OF CAIAPHAS TO THE SANHEDRIM CONCERNING THE EXECUTION OF JESUS.

RECORDS OF THE JERUSALEM SANHEDRIM, By ELIEZER HYRAN, B. 24.

TAKEN IN CONSTANTINOPLE, OCTOBER 16, 1883.

"*Caiaphas, Priest of the Most High God, to the Masters of Israel, greeting:* In obedience to your demands for a reason for my action in the case of Jesus of Nazareth, and in defense of my conduct, I beg leave to submit the following for your consideration : I would assure you that it was not on account of personal malice, envy, or hate, that existed in my own nature, nor for the want of a willingness upon my part to conform to the Jewish law in its strictest sense. I had but very little personal knowledge of the Nazarene. The most I knew of this man was from outside sources. Nor was it because he claimed to be King of the Jews, nor because he said he was the Son of God–I would that he were–nor because he prophesied or ignored the holy temple. No, nor all of these combined. There is a cause, and a more weighty matter, back of all these things that controlled my action in the matter. Therefore, I hope you will investigate strictly on legal principles the reasons that I may give.

"In order that you may be able to see and weigh the question fully, and remember the responsibility that rests upon me according to the laws of our Nation, I will ask you to go back with me to the chronicles of our history as a commonwealth. First, our faith is pledged to one living and true God, this God being indescribable, unchangeable, incomprehensible, and, of course, unnameable. But yet in our daily communications with, and our applications to Him, He has been pleased to give us His name, or His several names, according to His relations to us, and they are found nowhere, only in the ark of His holy temple—there where He presents to us His strength and power. He calls himself *Eloi*, which means almighty in strength ; that He can do what He will without effort ; that He does the greatest thing as easy as he does the least. This makes Him different from all beings. In His holy ark He records Himself *Elaah*—existence without beginning, and no contingency as to His end. Again, He writes Himself *Hhelejon*—unchangeable ; that is, nothing but His own will can change Him. Again, he records His name *Jah*—knowledge that comprehends without being comprehended. Again He is written *Adonai*—full and free, and freely full. Combining the several names we have *Jehovah*—the Hebrew God. A man never can go wrong while he can pronounce this name in its comprehensive sense. This is where the Zealots, the Sadducees, and Essenes had their origin, and it is the want of being able to pronounce this name in its comprehensive sense that causes so much dissension among us Jews. Jesus could pronounce this name, but he stole it out of the temple, as I am creditably informed.

"But the object in calling your attention to pronouncing this name, with all its bearings, may be seen if we turn to the third Book of Leviticus, section 10, wherein is the special order made by our God to Moses, that we should offer the bullock, the ram, the flour and oil, and the people should fast seven days, and this should be *kaphar,* or atonement for the sins of all the people. Now, unless Moses was deceived, he has deceived us, or Jesus of Nazareth is a false teacher; for all he teaches is *metanoeite, metanoeite,* as though a man's being sorry for a crime would make restitution to the offended party. A man might repent ever so much, but what good would that do toward healing the man he had injured ? None in the least. This mode of making atonement was ordained of God and revealed to Moses; but if man has nothing to do but to repent, the disease carries its own remedy with it. So a man can sin as often as he may wish to. Look at the first book, section 3 : 'And God said to Abraham, by his own mouth, that each and all that were circumcised by the cutting of the prepuce should be saved.' This should be the seal of the covenant. Now, if this is not true, God must go against His own contract, violate His own promises, as well as deceive the faith and cheat the obedience of His own children. This is all so, if Jesus's teaching be true, for he sets up *table* (baptism) as the seal of God. I refer you to section 10, division first, where God said to Moses that He had changed the laws, converted the elements for the protection of His people, and with His own arm had delivered them out of a strong compact; and that they might remember, and that the generation to be born might remember and never forget to trust in Him when in danger, He said that once every year we should roast a kid or lamb, and eat it with unleavened bread, and this should be the sign that we would trust in Him in all times of danger. Now Jesus teaches that common bread and wine are to be used instead thereof– a thing unheard of. And not only so, something that is altogether repugnant to God, and something that fosters drunkenness, and is well qualified to excite men's passions. And oh, ye Masters of Israel, but think once. Jesus calls himself the Son of God ; claims to have been born of *almah* (the Hebrew word for virgin); that he and his Father are one–they are equal. These things will establish the following conclusions: If he is right, his Father is false. If they were one, then their teachings would be one; and if his teachings are true, God's must be wrong, or there are not those perfections in Him that we learn in pronouncing His holy name. By tolerating the teachings of Jesus, we say to the Romans that all of our former teachings are false; that the Hebrew's God is not to be trusted ; that He is weak, wanting in forethought; that He is vacillating and not to be trusted, much less to be honored and obeyed. Thus the world will lose confidence in our God, and confidence in us as a religious people. This is impregnating the whole atmosphere with moral pollution. It does not only cut off, but blocks the way of all Jews from heaven ; and not only this, it excludes our hope in the salvation of our forefathers, who have obeyed God in His ordinances, believed in His promises, and shouted in the triumphs of a holy life for fourteen hundred years. He entirely ignores God's holy temple–the house God had built by our forefathers under His own supervision, where He promised to dwell with His children, to hear their prayers, and to be pleased with their sacrifices. This temple is the bond of the Jews. Here all men can come and be blessed. It is the earthly home of the souls of men–the place where men may hide from the storms of sin and persecution. This temple is where the foolish may learn wisdom, the place where the naked soul can be clothed, and where the hungry may be fed. This the grandest gift of our Father. Jesus completely ignores this temple; says the priests have made it a den of thieves; and sets up a sneer, and even scoffs at its sacred ordinances, and with a sort of selfish triumph says it shall be destroyed; and from his manner of saying it, I have no doubt he would be glad to see it quickly done. But what would be the condition of our people if this temple was removed? What would be the use of the priesthood if the temple was destroyed ? Where would we find an answer by Urim and Thummim ? How would the soul of man be purified, if the holy *Bath kole*, the *Euroch* of God should depart? There in that sacred temple of God he has been burning to the consuming of sin and the purifying of the heart since our return from bondage in Babylon. My argument is, if this temple is destroyed, or even forsaken by the Jews, we as a nation are utterly ruined. We might as well put our necks under the feet of idolatry and give up all hope.

"One more subject I place before my Masters of Israel. Is it compatible with our religion, or is it consistent with philosophy, or admitted in His holy

Word, that there can be more gods than one? When we pronounce *Ele Laah Shaddiai-Hhelyon Adonai* (which is *Jehovah*), there can be but one living God. By reference to section 6, No. four, He says by mouth of Moses, when he was all aglow with the glory of God–and remember He speaks either by mouth or quill; it is He that speaks, and not man–He says, 'The Lord your God is one God ; there can be but one. I am and have been with you ; I brought you up; I delivered you out of a strong compact; I delivered you out of their hand and kept you dry, while your enemies were drowned in the sea. I will not forsake you. I promised your father I would not. But if you forsake Me, then desolation will come upon you, and have you in swift destruction.' In section 5, three and four of David's Song of Joy: 'I am God alone. If I turn to the right or to the left, if I go down into the depths of the sea, or into the centre of the earth, or over the heavens, I should find no companion.' In section 3 He says : 'I am God alone, and alone I am God ; beside Me there is no help for man nor angels.' Then in section 13, this command has been given : 'Thou shall pay to the Lord thy God once a year a half-shekel of silver, that thou and thy children, and all the strangers that are within thy gate, may know that there is no God beside Me, on whom they may call in time of danger.' Now, having all these commands and teachings from the very lips of God himself before my eyes, and being held responsible for the soundness of our doctrine and the proper inculcation of the same among the people of the Jews, what was I to do? Could I stand as the priest of the Most High God, and see your blessed religion perverted by an impostor ? Could I stand and see the holy temple of our God deserted and forsaken? Could I stand and see all the holy ordinances, which had been appointed by our God for securing salvation to Israel, perverted by an impostor? All the blessed doctrines that were appointed for the government and instruction of the priesthood, thence to be imparted to the youth of our land, set aside, and that by one that could show no authority, only the authority of John the Baptist, who could give no authority only the one who sent him to baptize, and he could not tell who he was, nor whence he came ? Hence you can see the responsible position that I as the high priest of God and of the Jewish Church occupied. According to our laws I was made responsible, and stood between my God and my people, to protect them in doctrine and government. I refer you to the capitulation made by the Sanhedrim and Augustus Caesar, in the holy *Tosephta* of the Talmuds. We submitted to taxation by the Romans, and the Romans are to protect our holy religion from foreign foes, in order that the holy temple or any of its sacred ordinances should never be molested, nor the holy city, Jerusalem, be polluted by Roman idolatry. Now the insinuating plan adopted by Jesus was well qualified to deceive the common people. It had already led many to forsake the temple, and hold her ordinances in derision, as well as to neglect the teachings of the priest or to pay the tithes for their supplies. He had already inculcated into the Jewish mind his pernicious ways of being saved to that extent that the Jewish cause was almost lost. There are two reasons for this : First, the people to whom he preached were an ignorant set, and knew but very little about doctrine of any kind. They are a restless sort of men, who are always finding fault and wanting something new, and never associate with the more enlightened part of the community in order to learn. Another reason of his having many followers is, his doctrines are congenial to unsanctified flesh. They are so suited to human nature that they require no sacrifices; they need not go to the temple to worship God; they need not fast, and they can when and where they please ; they need pay no tithes to keep up the temple or the priesthood, but every man can be his own priest and worship God as he chooses. All this is so compatible with human nature that, although he has not been preaching over three years, he has more followers to-day than Abraham has, and they have become perfectly hostile toward the Jews that are faithful to their God ; and, if it had not been for the Roman soldiers, on the day of his execution we would have had one of the bloodiest insurrections ever known to the Jewish commonwealth. I am told that there was never seen such a concourse of people assembled at Jerusalem as at the cross. One of my guards informs me that there were several hundred thousand, and, although there were two others crucified at the same time, Jesus was the great centre of attraction. They would call out, 'Who is this Jesus of Nazareth? What is his crime?' Some of his friends would cry out, 'Nothing; he is being executed because he was a friend to the poor.' 'Take him down ! Take him down,' they would cry out, and the soldiers would have to use their spears to keep them back. But when he yielded up the ghost he proved to all that he was hypostatical (that is, a human body), and the *lodi curios* had come from the iclandic covenant, and his *trinitatis unitas* was all a sham, for how could this unpronounced name suffer or be captured by men, or die, unless he is the one that is to die for the many ? And if so, I was only accomplishing God's holy purposes, which exonerates me from guilt.

"But it seems to me a necessity that he should be removed. That this may be evident to your minds, I ask you to contrast our present condition with the past. Jesus of Nazareth spent two years in Egypt under the instruction of Rabbi Joshua, and learned the art of thaumaturgy to perfection, as has never been taught in any of the schools of necromancy among the heathen. If the healing miracles of Jesus are true, as they must be (for they are so acknowledged by his foes as well as his friends), he must have learned it from Horus and Serapis, as practised by those heathen priests. He came back to Palestine as a physician, and was by nature an enthusiast as well as a Hebrew patriarch, and when John's preaching excited idealistic minds, Jesus also went to that teacher, and was inspired by him to inculcate and promulgate his doctrines. Notwithstanding his youth and inexperience, Jesus started out as a public orator and teacher with the doctrines of John, and in that capacity referred exclusively to his authority, as every public teacher in these days has to be ordained by some acknowledged authority. As long as John was at large, Jesus in the capacity of an itinerant teacher and physician roused the people of Galilee to *metanoia* (repentance of sin), to bring about a restoration of the kingdom of heaven. He met with the same opposition that John did from those who would not admit that they were more sinful than their progenitors were, or that asceticism was the proper means for the restoration of the kingdom of heaven. But he met with the same success among the lower classes, such as foreign harlots, Sodomites, publicans, and other Roman agents, but the intelligent portion remained cold and unmoved by his enthusiasm. The cures which he performed appeared miraculous to his followers, but most ridiculous to the intelligent Jews and men of sober and reflective minds.

"Jesus embraced the humanitarian doctrine of the Hillelites, presenting conspicuously the cosmopolitan spirit of Judaism, and he did it almost in the words of Hillel, who had taught it before. Their faith and doctrine being alike, it was not hard for him to create excitement, or to find plenty of followers. In addition to all this, he taught a system of low morals, and so void of all ritualistic ideas that it was easy for him to get any number of followers. He taught the people that there was but one living and true God, but he taught them that he was that God, and that his father was merged into himself, and could not manifest himself only through him, which theory would confute itself if they would only stop to reflect, for as he was hypostatical or corporeal, his assistance was cut off from all that was not immediately in his presence, which is altogether incompatible with the faith of the Jews. Right in the face of this doctrine he would teach that there was a special providence, as well as a general providence, as if there could be a general providence without a God that could be present in all places at all times, as we learn in pronouncing His name. He taught that the dead will rise and live again in a future state of happiness or misery according as they have lived here. Therefore he taught future rewards and punishments; but he being present, how could he reward in the future? He taught the revelation and the prophets, but contradicted all they teach. He taught the election of Israel by the Almighty, but ignored all the doctrines of Israel. He taught the eternity of God's laws, and promises in the super-importance of the humanitarian over the ritual laws and doctrines, but I do not think he wished to abolish the latter, or even the traditional laws, but merely to supersede them by a higher life. The natural result of all this was that he disregarded the laws of Levitical cleanness, which were considered so important by the Shammaites and Essenes, and also by the Hillelites. This is the point where division commenced, and the breach grew wider and wider until an insurrection must have been the result. He so far cut himself loose from the Jews that he ate with unclean sinners, publicans, and lepers, and permitted harlots to touch him, while his disciples went so far as to eat their meals without washing themselves. Furthermore, he looked upon the whole of the Levitical institutions, temples, sacrifices, and priesthood included, as no longer necessary and not worth the life of the animal. This was certainly the opinion of the Hillelites. Jesus, it seems, found in this Hillelite school a party furnished to hand, ready to take up with his heresy (and a large party they are, almost sufficient to divide the whole Jewish commonwealth). They taught the repentance of sin, the practice of benevolence and charity, the education of the young, and good-will toward mankind, as possessing much more moral worth than all the Levitical cleanness, or compliance with the whole moral law given to us by our God to govern us. His preaching was of the parabolical style. He would rely on a text of scripture, for he seemed to hold the scriptures in high veneration, so his preaching was on the *midrash* style of the scribes–a maxim expressed in the style of Solon or of Sirach's son. His great object was to come as near the Jewish theology as possible so as to destroy the Jews' entirely, and establish his own. Hence he resorted to the allegorical method of the Egyptian Hebrews, uttering many good and wise sayings, which were not new to the learned, but which were taken from the common wisdom of the country, which was known by all who were acquainted with the literature of the rabbis. But they were new to his class of hearers, who were not accustomed to listen to the wise. He had no education, comparatively speaking. He was full of nervous excitement, all of which went to inspire his hearers with enthusiasm. He took but little care of his health or person ; cared not for his own relatives. He travelled mostly on foot in the company of his disciples and some suspicious women, and lived on the charity of his friends. He seemed to take no notice of the political affairs of his country ; would as soon be governed by one nation as another. In fact, it seemed if he had any preference it was for the Romans. It seems that he became so infatuated that he really thought he was the head of the kingdom of heaven. This manner of preaching, along with his presumption, aroused his enemies to a powerful pitch, and it was all I could do to keep the zealots from mobbing him in the temple. They had no confidence in a doctrine that set the Jewish laws at naught, and mocked the priesthood of God, and they with the Sadducees and scribes were not willing to submit to a man who acknowledged no authority higher than himself, and was seemingly endeavoring to overturn everything that they held more sacred and dearer than life. Jesus's mode and manner were well qualified to deceive the unsuspecting. 'Let us have all things in common,' said he, 'and he that would be greatest among you will prove his greatness by rendering the greatest service to all, and if any of the higher powers compel thee to go a mile, let him that is compelled go ten miles.' This caused him to be attacked more in his policy than in his doctrine. The great question with us Jews was, here are the Romans upon us; how can we get rid of them? Jesus's idea was to let the Romans alone; it matters not who rules and governs the nations; it they abuse you, love them in return, and they cannot be your enemies long; no man can continue to abuse another who returns injuries with love. Keep from them ; pray in secret for the return of the kingdom of heaven and God's grace, and this will soon make all things right. 'Pay your taxes,' he would say to them ; 'it is only Caesar's money you pay, which is unlawful for you to have–unlawful on account of its idolatrous effigies.' Again, he would say to his hearers, 'You cannot conquer the Romans ; better convert them, and they are your enemies no longer. They already have your temple in their possession ; their yoke is getting heavier every day, and the more you fight against them the more they will abuse you; therefore, your only chance is to love them, and try to make your yoke easy and your burden light by having them your friends.' Indeed, the conduct of Jesus was so strange and incompatible with the interest of the Jews as a nation, that it seemed to me that he was a subject employed by the Romans to keep the Jews submissive and obedient to all their tyranny and abuse.

"This policy was most powerfully attacked by the officiating priest, by the Shammaites and Zealots, and, in fact, the whole Jewish nation was becoming aroused to a war heat. The reprimands of Jesus were so severe against the rich and highly educated that they had turned against him, and brought all the power they had, both of their wealth and talent, so that I saw that a bloody insurrection was brewing fast. The public mind of the Jews was becoming more and more divided and corrupt; heretical doctrines were being diffused all over the land; the temple was forsaken and the holy sacraments neglected ; the people were dividing into sects, and these breaches were like a rent in a garment–tearing wider apart continually. As it seemed to me, the whole of the Jewish theocracy was about to be blown away as a bubble on a breaker.

"As the Jews became more and more divided and confused, the tyranny of the Romans increased. All they wanted was an excuse to slaughter the Jews and confiscate their property. At this time both the doctrine and religion of the Jews were spreading rapidly all over Rome, which gave the Romans great alarm. Sejane undertook to have an ordinance passed in the Senate, abolishing the Jewish religion from Rome; and when he found it would cause an insurrection, they banished all the Jews from Rome, and back they came to Judea with all their idolatry and heresy, and many other corrupt principles from the Romans, which fitted them to join any party for profit. Up to this time the Roman governors had shown great kindness to the Jews. There never was a better man than Hyrcan. The Jews enjoyed great peace during his administration. But Tiberias has turned against us; Pilate has removed the army from Caesarea to Jerusalem. I say, no nation with any self-respect, or one that had any energy left, would or could stand it without a struggle.

"Now, the preaching of John the Baptist and Jesus of Nazareth had brought all these things upon us. When Herod Antipas captured John, it quieted matters in Galilee, so that they had peace until Jesus started it up afresh. I had issued orders to Jesus to desist from preaching, unless he taught as the Jews taught. He sent me the impertinent word that his doctrine was not of this world, but had reference to the world to come; when he was all the time doing all he could to destroy the peace and harmony of this world. Now, according to our law in the *Saphra*, by Jose. B. Talmud, it devolves on me to see that the people have sound doctrine taught them. Hence it is my duty to examine all the *midrashim*, or sermons, of all the preaching priests, and if anyone teach the people wrongly, or if his conduct is not in correspondence with his profession, to cause him to desist ; or if any disregard the holy laws of ablution, or in any way defile himself, or if he shall be guilty of misconduct in any way, either in manner of life or doctrine, to adjudge such an one, and pronounce sentence for his crime upon him. This I did upon Jesus of Nazareth, to save the Church from heresy, and to save the cause of the Jewish commonwealth from final ruin. But understand that I did not act rashly nor illegally, as I am accused. I only passed sentence under the protest and order of the whole court belonging to the high priest, containing twelve members, or elders, and priests. Thus you will see it was not my voluntary act, but was a legal one and in accordance with law. After I examined Jesus on the various charges, he said in the presence of all the court that each and all of them were true. I then reasoned with him and asked him, if the court of the high priest would forgive him of these charges would he desist from these things in all time to come. He answered most emphatically and positively he would not. Under these circumstances I was compelled, according to our law, to sentence him to die ; for if he continued to promulgate his pernicious heresies the Jews, as a nation, must perish with their religion. And, as you find in the *Tosephta,* that the nation has always the right of self-preservation, and as we had conceded the right to the Romans of executing our criminal laws, it became my painful duty to send him to Pontius Pilate, with the following charges:

"*Caiaphas, High Priest of the Most High God, to Pontius Pilate, Governor of the Roman Province:*
"Jesus of Nazareth is thus charged by the High Court of the Jews :
" 'First, with teaching the doctrine that there are more gods than one, which is contrary to the teachings of the Jewish law, which he most positively refuses to

desist from in the presence of this court.

" 'Second, he teaches that he is a God, which is contrary to the Jewish law, and he is visible and comprehensible; and, after being asked to desist by this court, he most positively affirms that he is the Son of God.

" 'Third, he teaches and affirms that the *Bath kole* (Holy Spirit) cannot come until he goes away, which is contrary to the teachings of the Jews ; because it was He that brooded over the waters, and has been in the habitual light of the world ever since; from all of which he refuses to desist.

" 'He teaches baptism as the seal of God, instead of circumcision, which was established by the decrees of God with Abraham as a seal of the Jews; and when abjured to desist by this court declared he would not.

" 'He teaches asceticism as the means of salvation, contrary to the Jewish custom ; and affirmed in the presence of this court he would not desist.

" 'He teaches that the Levitical ablution is of no service, while we hold that the outward washing is the sign of inward purity; and when abjured to desist he emphatically refused.

" 'He has abrogated the ordinance given by God to Moses of the pascal supper, wherein we should roast a lamb and eat it with unleavened bread ; but Jesus has introduced a custom altogether different–without any authority. He has introduced common bread and wine, which are not only forbidden, but are well qualified to excite men's passions and make them forget God rather than to remember and trust Him, this feast having been introduced that we should remember to trust Him in the hours of trouble. When asked why he did this, all he would say was: "Hitherto I work, and my Father works."

" 'He has abrogated the priesthood, and set the temple at naught, which is the very life's blood of the Jewish faith.

" 'Were it not that God our Father has given us these holy ordinances we would not be so tenacious of them. We know they are the pillars upon which the Jewish theocracy is built, and that we cannot live without them. Although Jesus of Nazareth has been abjured time and again to stop teaching these ways of death, he has as often declared he would not; therefore it devolves on me as the proper and the only officer to pronounce sentence upon him.'

"These charges were written by my scribe, and sent with the officers to Pilate for his consent. Of course, I did not expect him to execute him as he did, but it seems that the mob was so great that Pilate never received them. I expected Pilate to send Jesus back to me, so that I could send him to you for your approval; and if so, then I would proceed to try him with Urim and Thummim, with the regular *lacktees* on guard, as our law requires; but it seems that Pilate thirsted for his blood. Like all guilty tyrants, he was afraid of his own shadow, and wished to destroy everything that threatened his power.

"With these reasons for my actions, I submit the case which I am sure will be considered favorably by my Masters of Israel."

CHAPTER VII.

REPORT OF CAIAPHAS TO THE SANHEDRIM CONCERNING THE RESURRECTION OF JESUS.

After having made the preceding record of Caiaphas, on unwinding the same scroll we found another report from him. It may be interesting to the reader to know what we mean by a scroll. It is similar to parchment. The Hebrew word *numet* means a pulp made from the bark of the reed into a paste, and dried in the sun until it is hard ; when pressed and polished it shines beautifully, and its surface is as smooth as our paper. It is of two kinds: one is called *papyrus*, the other *hierotike*. The latter is more costly, and is used by priests alone. It is about sixteen inches wide, and is cemented together by a gum that exudes from a tree resembling our elm. It is written upon with some kind of indelible ink or paint, with a common reed quill, which is fashioned like our pens. The writing is done by the *sopher,* which is the Hebrew word for scribe. He is called *grammateus* by the Greeks. The report of Caiaphas is written in what is known as the square Hebrew. The letters are from a half-inch to an inch in size, so that one can imagine what a roll of parchment it would take to record a deed. It is read only with difficulty by the best Hebrew scholars, and they must have text-books to assist them. But after one has gotten the thread of the subject he can get along with it. This is the reason I got Dr. McIntosh to go with me. He and

Dr. Twyman have been in the business for many years. The windlass, as it might be called (for it more resembles our common rope-winders than anything I can think of), is a square piece of timber, about three inches in diameter, to which the scroll is fastened at one end, around which it is rolled like a spool. At the proper distance are tied two transverse sticks to hold the parchment to its proper place. The windlass with the scroll is placed at one end of a table, and an empty windlass at the other end, so that as you unwind from the one to read, the scroll winds around the other. The letters are very distinct. There are hundreds of these arranged in rows. They are all lettered and numbered with their dates on them. This makes it easy to find anything desired. There is another class of books of fine sheep or goat skin, about eight by twelve inches. The writing on these is very fine and difficult to read. They are bound between cedar boards, with clasps, and contain from eight to forty sheets to the book. These are the kind of books of which Josephus wrote seventy-two.

But to return to Caiaphas's report. After unwinding several feet, as before stated, we came across another communication from Caiaphas; I hardly know whether to call it a resignation or a confession.

One thing I do know, it is one of the most solemn things that I have ever read. We thanked God that we had come to Constantinople, and that Mohammed had given orders to preserve these sacred scrolls in the mosque of St. Sophia. It is as follows:

"*Sanhedrim, 89. By Siphri 11, 7.*:

"*To You, Masters of Israel:* As I have made a

former defence to you, and you have approved the same, I feel in duty bound to communicate to you some facts that have come to my knowledge since that communication. A few days after the execution ,of Jesus of Nazareth the report of his resurrection from the dead became so common that I found it necessary to investigate it, because the excitement was more intense than before, and my own life as well as that of Pilate was in danger. I sent for Malkus, the captain of the royal city guard, who informed me he knew nothing personally, as he had placed Isham in command of the guard ; but from what he could learn from the soldiers the scene was awe-inspiring, and the report was so generally believed that it was useless to deny it. He thought my only chance was to suppress it among the soldiers, and have John and Peter banished to Crete, or arrested and imprisoned, and if they would not be quiet, to treat them as I had treated Jesus. He said that all the soldiers he had conversed with were convinced that Jesus was resurrected by supernatural power and was still living, and that he was no human being, for the light and the angels and the dead that came out of their graves all went to prove that something had happened that never occurred on earth before. He said that John and Peter were spreading it all over the country, and that if Jesus would appear at the head of a host, and declare for the king of the Jews, he believed all the Jews would fight for him. I sent for the lieutenant, who gave a lengthy account of the occurrence that morning, all of which I suppose you have learned, and will investigate. From this I am convinced that something transcending the laws of nature took place that morning, that cannot be accounted for upon natural laws, and I find it is useless to try to get any of the soldiers to deny it, for they are so excited that they cannot be reasoned with. I regret that I had the soldiers placed at the tomb, for the very things that they were to prevent they have helped to establish.

"After questioning the soldiers and officers to my satisfaction, My mind being so disturbed that I could neither eat nor sleep, I sent for John and Peter. They came and brought Mary and Joanna, who are the women that went to embalm Jesus's body the morning of the resurrection, as it is called. They were very interesting as they related the circumstances. Mary says that when they went day was just breaking. They met the soldiers returning from the sepulchre, and saw nothing strange until they came to the tomb, and found that it was empty. The stone that covered the sepulchre was rolled to one side, and two men dressed in flowing white were sitting, one at each end of the sepulchre. Mary asked them where was her Lord ; they said, 'He is risen from the dead; did he not tell you he would rise the third day and show himself to the people, to prove that he was the Lord of life?' Go tell his disciples, said they. Joanna said she saw but one man ; but this discrepancy must have been due to their excitement, because they say they were much alarmed. They both say that as they returned they met the Master, who told them that he was the resurrection and the life; all that will accept shall be resurrected from the second death. 'We fell at his feet, all bathed in tears, and when we rose up he was gone.' Both these women wept for joy while relating these circumstances, and John shouted aloud, which made me tremble in every limb, for I could not help thinking that something that was the exclusive work of God had occurred, but what it all meant was a great mystery to me. It might be, I said, that God had sent this message by the mouth of this stranger ; it might be that he was the seed of the woman, and we his people had executed him.

"I asked John and Peter if they could give me any further evidence in regard to this man ; that I wished to be informed of his private history. Peter said that Jesus passed by where he was, and bade him follow him, and he felt attracted to him, but at first it was more through curiosity than anything in the man ; that he soon became acquainted with Mary, who told him that he was her son, and related to him the strange circumstances of his birth, and that she was convinced that he was to be the king of the Jews. She spoke of many strange things concerning his life, which made Peter feel more interested in him than he would have been otherwise. He said that Jesus was a man so pleasant in his character, and so like a child in innocence, that no one could help liking him after he got acquainted with him; that though he seemed to be stern and cold, he was not so in reality ; that he was exceedingly kind, especially to the poor; that he would make any sacrifice for the sick and needy, and would spare no effort to impart knowledge to anyone that would call on him, and that his knowledge was so profound that he had seen him interrogated by the most learned doctors of the law, and he always gave the most perfect satisfaction, and that the *sopher* or scribes, and the Hillelites, and Shammaites were afraid to open their mouths in his presence. They had attacked him so often and been repelled that they shunned him as they would a wolf; but when he had repelled them he did not enjoy the triumph as they did over others of whom they had gotten the ascendancy. As to his private life, he seemed not to be a man of pleasure, nor of sorrow. He mingled with society to benefit it, and yet took no part at all in what was going on. 'I had heard many tell of what occurred when he was baptized, and from what his mother told me I was watching for a display of his divine power, if he had any, for I knew he could never be king of the Jews unless he did have help from on high. Once when we were attending a marriage-feast the wine gave out, and his mother told him of it, and he said to the men to fill up some water-pots that were sitting near, and they put in nothing but water, for I watched them, but when they poured it out it was wine, for it was tasted by all at the feast, and when the master found it out he called for Jesus to honor him, but he had disappeared. It seemed that he did not want to be popular, and this spirit displeased us, for we knew if he was to be king of the Jews he must become popular with the Jews. His behavior angered his mother, for she was doing all she could to bring him into notice, and to make him popular among the people, and the people could not help liking him when they saw him. Another peculiarity was that in his presence everyone felt safe. There seemed to be an almighty power pervading the air wherever he went so that everyone felt secure, and believed that no harm could befall them if Jesus were present. As we were in our fishing-boat I saw Jesus coming out toward us, walking on the water.

I knew that if he could make the waves support him, he could me also. I asked him if I might come to him ; he said to me to come, but when I saw the waves gathering around me I began to sink, and asked him to help me. He lifted me up, and told me to have faith in God. On another occasion we were sailing on the sea, and there was a great storm. It blew at a fearful rate, and all on board thought they would be lost; we awakened the master, and when he saw the raging of the storm he stretched out his hand and said, "Peace, be still !" and the wind ceased to blow, the thunder stopped, the lightnings withdrew, and the billowing sea seemed as quiet as a babe in its mother's arms–all done in one moment of time. This I saw with my own eyes, and from that time I was convinced that he was not a common man. Neither did he work by enchantment like the Egyptian thaumaturgists, for in all their tricks they never attack the laws of nature. In vain might they order the thunder to hush, or the winds to abate, or the lightnings to cease their flashing. Again, I saw this man while we were passing from Jericho. There was a blind man, who cried out to him for mercy, and Jesus said to me, "Go, bring him near," and when I brought him near Jesus asked him what he wanted. He said he wanted to see him. Jesus said, "Receive thy sight," when he was not near enough for Jesus to lay his hands upon him or use any art. Thus were all his miracles performed. He did not act as the Egyptian necromancers. They use vessels, such as cups, bags, and jugs, and many other things to deceive. Jesus used nothing but his simple speech in such a way that all could understand him, and it seemed as if the laws of nature were his main instruments of action, and that nature was as obedient to him as a slave is to his master. I recall another occasion when a young man was dead, and Jesus loved his sisters. One of them went with Jesus to the tomb. He commanded it to be uncovered. The sister said, "Master, by this time he is offensive ; he has been dead four days." Jesus said, "Only have faith," and he called the young man by name, and he came forth out of the tomb, and is living to-day,' and Peter proposed that I should see him for myself.

"Thus argue Peter and John. If Jesus had such power over nature and nature's laws, and power over death in others, he would have such power over death that he could lay down his life and take it up again, as he said he would do. As he proposes to bring hundreds of witnesses to prove all he says, and much more—witnesses whose veracity cannot be doubted—and as I had heard many of these things before from different men, both friends and foes (and although these things are related by his friends—that is, the friends of Jesus—yet these men talk like men of truth, and their testimony corroborates other evidence that I have from other sources, that convinces me that this is something that should not be rashly dealt with), and seeing the humble trust and confidence of these men and women, besides, as John says, thousands of others equally strong in their belief, it throws me into great agitation. I feel some dreadful foreboding—a weight upon my heart. I cannot feel as a criminal from the fact that I was acting according to my best judgment with the evidence before me. I feel that I was acting in defence of God and my country, which I love better than my life, and if I was mistaken, I was honest in my mistake. And as we teach that honesty of purpose gives character to the action, on this basis I shall try to clear myself of any charge, yet there is a conscious fear about my heart, so that I have no rest day or night. I feel sure that if I should meet Jesus I would fall dead at his feet ; and it seemed to me if I went out I would be sure to meet him.

"In this state of conscious dread I remained investigating the Scriptures to know more about the prophecies concerning this man, but found I nothing to satisfy my mind. I locked my door and gave the guards orders to let no one in without first giving me notice. While thus engaged, with no one in the room but my wife and Annas, her father, when I lifted up my eyes, behold Jesus of Nazareth stood before me. My breath stopped, my blood ran cold and I was in the act of falling, when he spoke and said, 'Be not afraid, it is I. You condemned me that you might go free. This is the work of my Father. Your only wrong is, you have a wicked heart; this you must repent of. This last lamb you have slain is the one that was appointed before the foundation ; this sacrifice is made for all men. Your other lambs were for those who offered them ; this is for all, this is the last ; it is for you if you will accept it. I died that you and all in the world might be saved.' At this he looked at me with melting tenderness that it seemed to me I was nothing but tears, and my strength was all gone. I fell on my face at his feet as one that was dead. When Annas lifted me up Jesus was gone, and the door still locked. No one could tell when or where he went.

"So, noble Masters, I do not feel that I can officiate as priest any more. If this strange personage is from God, and should prove to be the Saviour we have looked for so long, and I have been the means of crucifying him, I have no further offerings to make for sin ; but I will wait and see how these things will develop. And if he proves to be the ruler that we are looking for, they will soon develop into something more grand in the future. His glory will increase; his influence will spread wider and wider, until the whole earth shall be full of his glory, and all the kingdoms of the world shall be his dominion. Such are the teachings of the prophets on this subject. Therefore you will appoint Jonathan, or some one, to fill the holy place."

[We found that, soon after, Jonathan became high priest, though history teaches us differently.–MAHAN.]

CHAPTER VIII.

VALLEUS'S NOTES.–ACTA PILATI, OR PILATE'S REPORT TO CAESAR OF THE ARREST, TRIAL, AND CRUCIFIXION OF JESUS.

VALLEUS PATERCULUS, a Roman historian, was nineteen years old when Jesus was born, His works have been thought to be extinct. I know of but two historians that make reference to his writings, Priscian and Tacitus, who speak of him as a descendant of an equestrian family of Campania. From what we gather from these writers, Valleus must have been a close friend of Caesar, who raised him by degrees until he became one of the great men of Rome, and for sixteen years commanded the army. He returned to Rome in the year 31 and finished his work, which was called *Historia Romania.* He held the office of praetor when Augustus died, and while Vinceus was consul.

Valleus says that in Judea he met a man called Jesus of Nazareth, who was one of the most remarkable characters he had ever seen ; that he was more afraid of Jesus than of a whole army, for he cured all manner of diseases and raised the dead, and when he cursed the orchards or fruit-trees for their barrenness, they instantly withered to their roots. After referring to the wonderful works of Jesus, he says that, although Jesus had such power, he did not use it to injure any one, but seemed always inclined to help the poor. Valleus says the Jews were divided in their opinion of him, the poorer class claiming him as their king and their deliverer from Roman authority, and that if Jesus should raise an army and give it the power he could sweep the world in a single day ; but the rich Jews hated and cursed him behind his back, and called him an Egyptian necromancer, though they were as afraid of him as of death (*Valleus Paterculus*, B. 72, found in the Vatican at Rome).

PILATE'S REPORT.

"To TIBERIUS CAESAR, EMPEROR OF ROME.

"*Noble Sovereign, Greeting :* The events of the last few days in my province have been of such a character that I will give the details in full as they occurred, as I should not be surprised if, in the course of time, they may change the destiny of our nation, for it seems of late that all the gods have ceased to be propitious. I am almost ready to say, Cursed be the day that I succeeded Vallerius Flaceus in the government of Judea; for since then my life has been one of continual uneasiness and distress.

"On my arrival at Jerusalem I took possession of the praetorium, and ordered a splendid feast to be prepared, to which I invited the tetrarch of Galilee, with the high priest and his officers. At the appointed hour no guests appeared. This I considered an insult offered to my dignity, and to the whole government which I represent. A few days after the high priest deigned to pay me a visit. His deportment was grave and deceitful. He pretended that his religion forbade him and his attendants to sit at the table of the Romans, and eat and offer libations with them, but this was only a sanctimonious seeming, for his very countenance betrayed his hypocrisy. Although I thought it expedient to accept his excuse, from that moment I was convinced that the conquered had declared themselves the enemy of the conquerors ; and I would warn the Romans to beware of the high priests of this country. They would betray their own mother to gain office and a luxurious living. It seems to me that, of conquered cities, Jerusalem is the most difficult to govern. So turbulent are the people that I live in momentary dread of an insurrection. I have not soldiers sufficient to suppress it. I had only one centurion and a hundred men at my command. I requested a reinforcement from the prefect of Syria, who informed me that he had scarcely troops sufficient to defend his own province. An insatiate thirst for conquest to extend our empire beyond the means of defending it, I fear, will be the cause of the final overthrow of our whole government. I lived secluded from the masses, for I did not know what those priests might influence the rabble to do ; yet I endeavored to ascertain, as far as I could, the mind and standing of the people.

"Among the various rumors that came to my ears there was one in particular that attracted my attention. A young man, it was said, had appeared in Galilee preaching with a noble unction a new law in the name of the God that had sent him. At first I was apprehensive that his design was to stir up the people against the Romans, but my fears were soon dispelled.

Jesus of Nazareth spoke rather as friend of the Romans than of the Jews. One day in passing by the place of Siloe, where there was a great concourse of people, I observed in the midst of the group a young man who was leaning against a tree, calmly addressing the multitude. I was told it was Jesus. This I could easily have suspected, so great was the difference between him and those listening to him. His golden-colored hair and beard gave to his appearance a celestial aspect. He appeared to be about thirty years of age. Never have I seen a sweeter or more serene countenance. What a contrast between him and his hearers, with their black beards and tawny complexions!

"Unwilling to interrupt him by my presence, I continued my walk, but signified to my secretary to join the group and listen. My secretary's name is Manlius. He is the grandson of the chief of the conspirators who encamped in Etruria waiting for Cataline. Manlius had been for a long time an inhabitant of Judea, and is well acquainted with the Hebrew language. He was devoted to me, and worthy of my confidence. On entering the praetorium I found Manlius, who related to me the words Jesus had pronounced at Siloe. Never have I read in the works of the philosophers anything that can compare to the maxims of Jesus. One of the rebellious Jews, so numerous in Jerusalem, having asked Jesus if it was lawful to give tribute to Caesar, he replied: 'Render unto Caesar the things that belong to Caesar, and unto God the things that are God's.'

"It was on account of the wisdom of his sayings that I granted so much liberty to the Nazarene; for it was in my power to have had him arrested, and exiled to Pontus; but that would have been contrary to the justice which has always characterized the Roman government in all its dealings with men ; this man was neither seditious nor rebellious ; I extended to him my protection, unknown perhaps to himself. He was at liberty to act, to speak, to assemble and address the people, and to choose disciples, unrestrained by any praetorian mandate. Should it ever happen (may the gods avert the omen!), should it ever happen, I say, that the religion of our forefathers will be supplanted by the religion of Jesus, it will be to this noble toleration that Rome shall owe her premature death, while I, miserable wretch, will have been the instrument of what the Jews call Providence, and we call destiny.

"This unlimited freedom granted to Jesus provoked the Jews–not the poor, but the rich and powerful. It is true, Jesus was severe on the latter, and this was a political reason, in my opinion, for not restraining the liberty of the Nazarene. 'Scribes and Pharisees,' he would say to them, 'you are a race of vipers; you resemble painted sepulchres; you appear well unto men, but you have death within you.' At other times he would sneer at the alms of the rich and proud, telling them that the mite of the poor was more precious in the sight of God. Complaints were daily made at the praetorium against the insolence of Jesus.

"I was even informed that some misfortune would befall him ; that it would not be the first time that Jerusalem had stoned those who called themselves prophets; an appeal would be made to Caesar. However, my conduct was approved by the Senate, and I was promised a reinforcement after the termination of the Parthian war.

"Being too weak to suppress an insurrection, I resolved upon adopting a measure that promised to restore the tranquillity of the city without subjecting the praetorium to humiliating concessions. I wrote to Jesus requesting an interview with him at the praetorium. He came. You know that in my veins flows the Spanish mixed with Roman blood–as incapable of fear as it is of weak emotion. When the Nazarene made his appearance, I was walking in my basilic, and my feet seemed fastened with an iron hand to the marble pavement, and I trembled in every limb as does a guilty culprit, though the Nazarene was as calm as innocence itself. When he came up to me he stopped, and by a signal sign he seemed to say to me, 'I am here,' though he spoke not a word.

For some time I contemplated with admiration and awe this extraordinary type of man–a type of man unknown to our numerous painters, who have given form and figure to all the gods and the heroes. There was nothing about him that was repelling in its character, yet I felt too awed and tremulous to approach him.

" 'Jesus,' said I unto him at last–and my tongue faltered–' Jesus of Nazareth, for the last three years I have granted you ample freedom of speech ; nor do I regret it. Your words are those of a sage. I know not whether you have read Socrates or Plato, but this I know, there is in your discourses a majestic simplicity that elevates you far above those philosophers. The Emperor is informed of it, and I, his humble representative in this country, am glad of having allowed you that liberty of which you are so worthy. However, I must not conceal from you that your discourses have raised up against you powerful and inveterate enemies. Nor is this surprising. Socrates had his enemies, and he fell a victim to their hatred. Yours are doubly incensed–against you on account of your discourses being so severe upon their conduct ; against me on account of the liberty I have afforded you. They even accuse me of being indirectly leagued with you for the purpose of depriving the Hebrews of the little civil power which Rome has left them. My request–I do not say my order–is, that you be more circumspect and moderate in your discourses in the future, and more considerate of them, lest you arouse the pride of your enemies, and they raise against you the stupid populace, and compel me to employ the instruments of law.'

"The Nazarene calmly replied: 'Prince of the earth, your words proceed not from true wisdom. 'Say to the torrent to stop in the midst of the mountain-gorge : it will uproot the trees of the valley. The torrent will answer you that it obeys the laws of nature and the Creator. God alone knows whither flow the waters of the torrent. Verily I say unto you, before the rose of Sharon blossoms the blood of the just shall be spilt.'

"'Your blood shall not be spilt,' said I, with deep emotion ; 'you are more precious in my estimation on account of your wisdom than all the turbulent and proud Pharisees who abuse the freedom granted them by the Romans. They conspire against Caesar, and convert his bounty into fear, impressing the unlearned that Caesar is a tyrant and seeks their ruin. Insolent wretches! they are not aware that the wolf of the Tiber sometimes clothes himself with the skin of the sheep to accomplish his wicked designs. I will protect you against them. My praetorium shall be an asylum, sacred both day and night.'

Jesus carelessly shook his head, and said with a grave and divine smile : 'When the day shall have come there will be no asylums for the son of man, neither in the earth nor under the earth. The asylum of the just is there,' pointing to the heavens. 'That which is written in the books of the prophets must be accomplished.'

" 'Young man,' I answered, mildly, you will oblige me to convert my request into an order. The safety of the province which has been confided to my care requires it. You must observe more moderation in your discourses. Do not infringe my order. You know the consequences. May happiness attend you ; farewell.'

" 'Prince of the earth,' replied Jesus, ' I come not to bring war into the world, but peace, love, and charity. I was born the same day on which Augustus Caesar gave peace to the Roman world. Persecutions proceed not from me. I expect it from others, and will meet it in obedience to the will of my Father, who has shown me the way. Restrain, therefore, your worldly prudence. It is not in your power to arrest the victim at the foot of the tabernacle of expiation.'

"So saying, he disappeared like a bright shadow behind the curtains of the basilic–to my great relief, for I felt a heavy burden on me, of which I could not relieve myself while in his presence.

"To Herod, who then reigned in Galilee, the enemies of Jesus addressed themselves, to wreak their vengeance on the Nazarene. Had Herod consulted his own inclinations, he would have ordered Jesus immediately to be put to death; but, though proud of his royal dignity, yet he hesitated to commit an act that might lessen his influence with the Senate, or, like me, was afraid of Jesus. But it would never do for a Roman officer to be scared by a Jew. Previously to this, Herod called on me at the praetorium, and, on rising to take leave, after some trifling conversation, asked me what was my opinion concerning the Nazarene. I replied that Jesus appeared to me to be one of those great philosophers that great nations sometimes produced; that his doctrines were by no means sacrilegious, and that the intentions of Rome were to leave him to that freedom of speech which was justified by his actions. Herod smiled maliciously, and, saluting me with ironical respect, departed.

"The great feast of the Jews was approaching, and the intention was to avail themselves of the popular exultation which always manifests itself at the solemnities of a passover. The city was overflowing with a tumultuous populace, clamoring for the death of the Nazarene. My emissaries informed me that the treasure of the temple had been employed in bribing the people. The danger was pressing. A Roman centurion had been insulted. I wrote to the Prefect of Syria for a hundred foot soldiers and as many cavalry. He declined. I saw myself alone with a handful of veterans in the midst of a rebellious city, too weak to suppress an uprising, and having no choice left but to tolerate it. They had seized upon Jesus, and the seditious rabble, although they had nothing to fear from the praetorium, believing, as their leaders had told them, that I winked at their sedition—continued vociferating : Crucify him ! Crucify him!'

"Three powerful parties had combined together at that time against Jesus: First, the Herodians and the Sadducees, whose seditious conduct seemed to have proceeded from double motives : they hated the Nazarene and were impatient of the Roman yoke. They never forgave me for having entered the holy city with banners that bore the image of the Roman emperor; and although in this instance I had committed a fatal error, yet the sacrilege did not appear less heinous in their eyes. Another grievance also rankled in their bosoms. I had proposed to employ a part of the treasure of the temple in erecting edifices for public use. My proposal was scorned. The Pharisees were the avowed enemies of Jesus. They cared not for the government. They bore with bitterness the severe reprimands which the Nazarene for three years had been continually giving them wherever he went. Timid and too weak to act by themselves, they had embraced the quarrels of the Herodians and the Sadducees. Besides these three parties, I had to contend against the reckless and profligate populace, always ready to join a sedition, and to profit by the disorder and confusion that resulted therefrom.

"Jesus was dragged before the High Priest and condemned to death. It was then that the High Priest, Caiaphas, performed a divisory act of submission. He sent his prisoner to me to confirm his condemnation and secure his execution. I answered him that, as Jesus was a Galilean, the affair came under Herod's jurisdiction, and ordered him to be sent thither. The wily tetrarch professed humility, and, protesting his deference to the lieutenant of Caesar, he committed the fate of the man to my hands. Soon my palace assumed the aspect of a besieged citadel. Every moment increased the number of the malcontents. Jerusalem was inundated with crowds from the mountains of Nazareth. All Judea appeared to be pouring into the city.

I had taken a wife from among the Gauls, who pretended to see into futurity. Weeping and throwing herself at my feet she said to me: 'Beware, beware, and touch not that man ; for he is holy. Last night I saw him in a vision. He was walking on the waters ; he was flying on the wings of the wind. He spoke to the tempest and to the fishes of the lake ; all were obedient to him. Behold, the torrent in Mount Kedron flows with blood, the statues of Caesar are filled with gemonide; the columns of the interium have given away, and the sun is veiled in mourning like a vestal in the tomb. Ah ! Pilate, evil awaits thee. If thou wilt not listen to the vows of thy wife, dread the curse of a Roman Senate ; dread the frowns of Caesar.'

"By this time the marble stairs groaned under the weight of the multitude. The Nazarene was brought back to me. I proceeded to the halls of justice, followed by my guard, and asked the people in a severe tone what they demanded.

"'The death of the Nazarene,' was the reply.

"'For what crime ?'

"'He has blasphemed; he has prophesied the ruin of the temple ; he calls himself the Son of God, the

Messiah, the King of the Jews.'

"'Roman justice,' said I, 'punishes not such offences with death.'

"'Crucify him ! Crucify him!' cried the relentless rabble. The vociferations of the infuriated mob shook the palace to its foundations.

" There was but one who appeared to be calm in the midst of the vast multitude ; it was the Nazarene. After many fruitless attempts to protect him from the fury of his merciless persecutors, I adopted a measure which at the moment appeared to me to be the only one that could save his life. I proposed, as it was their custom to deliver a prisoner on such occasions, to release Jesus and let him go free, that he might be the scapegoat, as they called it ; but they said Jesus must be crucified. I then spoke to them of the inconsistency of their course as being incompatible with their laws, showing that no criminal judge could pass sentence on a criminal unless he had fasted one whole day; and that the sentence must have the consent of the Sanhedrim, and the signature of the president of that court ; that no criminal could be executed on the same day his sentence was fixed, and the next day, on the day of his execution, the Sanhedrim was required to review the whole proceeding; also, according to their law, a man was stationed at the door of the court with a flag, and another a short way off on horseback to cry the name of the criminal and his crime, and the names of his witnesses, and to know if any one could testify in his favor; and the prisoner on his way to execution had the right to turn back three times, and to plead any new thing in his favor. I urged all these pleas, hoping they might awe them into subjection ; but they still cried, 'Crucify him ! Crucify him !'

"I then ordered Jesus to be scourged, hoping this might satisfy them ; but it only increased their fury. I then called for a basin, and washed my hands in the presence of the clamorous multitude, thus testifying that in my judgment Jesus of Nazareth had done nothing deserving of death ; but in vain. It was his life these wretches thirsted for.

"Often in our civil commotions have I witnessed the furious anger of the multitude, but nothing could be compared to what I witnessed on this occasion. It might have been truly said that all the phantoms of the infernal regions had assembled at Jerusalem. The crowd appeared not to walk, but to be borne off and whirled as a vortex, rolling along in living waves from the portals of the praetorium even unto Mount Zion, with howling screams, shrieks, and vociferations such as were never heard in the seditions of the Pannonia, or in the tumults of the forum.

"By degrees the day darkened like a winter's twilight, such as had been at the death of the great Julius Caesar. It was likewise the Ides of March. I, the continued governor of a rebellious province, was leaning against a column of my basilic, contemplating athwart the dreary gloom these fiends of Tartarus dragging to execution the innocent Nazarene. All around me was deserted. Jerusalem had vomited forth her indwellers through the funeral gate that leads to Gemonica. An air of desolation and sadness enveloped me. My guards had joined the cavalry, and the centurion, with a display of power, was endeavoring to keep order. I was left alone, and my breaking heart admonished me that what was passing at that moment appertained rather to the history of the gods than that of men. A loud clamor was heard proceeding from Golgotha, which, borne on the winds, seemed to announce an agony such as was never heard by mortal ears. Dark clouds lowered over the pinnacle of the temple, and setting over the city covered it as with a veil. So dreadful were the signs that men saw both in the heavens and on the earth that Dionysus the Areopagite is reported to have exclaimed, 'Either the author of nature is suffering or the universe is falling apart.'

"Whilst these appalling scenes of nature were transpiring, there was a dreadful earthquake in lower Egypt, which filled everybody with fear, and scared the superstitious Jews almost to death. It is said Balthasar, an aged and learned Jew of Antioch, was found dead after the excitement was over. Whether he died from alarm or grief is not known. He was a strong friend of the Nazarene.

"Near the first hour of the night I threw my mantle around me, and went down into the city toward the gates of Golgotha. The sacrifice was consummated. The crowd was returning home, still agitated, it is true, but gloomy, taciturn, and desperate. What they had witnessed had stricken them with terror and remorse. I also saw my little Roman cohort pass by mournfully, the standard-bearer having veiled his eagle in token of grief ; and I overheard some of the Jewish soldiers murmuring strange words which I did not understand. Others were recounting miracles very like those which have so often smitten the Romans by the will of the gods. Sometimes groups of men and women would halt, then, looking back toward Mount Calvary, would remain motionless in expectation of witnessing some new prodigy.

"I returned to the praetorium, sad and pensive. On ascending the stairs, the steps of which were still stained with the blood of the Nazarene, I perceived an old man in a suppliant posture, and behind him several Romans in tears. He threw himself at my feet and wept most bitterly. It is painful to see an old man weep, and my heart being already overcharged with grief, we, though strangers, wept together. And in truth it seemed that the tears lay very shallow that day with many whom I perceived in the vast concourse of people. I never witnessed such an extreme revulsion of feeling. Those who betrayed and sold him, those who testified against him, those who cried, 'Crucify him, we have his blood,' all slunk off like cowardly curs, and washed their teeth with vinegar. As I am told that Jesus taught a resurrection and a separation after death, if such should be the fact I am sure it commenced in this vast crowd.

" 'Father,' said I to him, after gaining control of my feelings, 'who are you, and what is your request?'

"' I am Joseph of Arimathaea,' replied he, 'and am come to beg of you upon my knees the permission to bury Jesus of Nazareth.'

" 'Your prayer is granted,' said I to him ; and at the same time I ordered Manlius to take some soldiers with him to superintend the interment, lest it should be profaned.

"A few days after the sepulchre was found empty. His disciples proclaimed all over the country that Jesus had risen from the dead, as he had foretold. This created more excitement even than the crucifixion. As to its truth I cannot say for certain, but I have made some investigation of the matter; so you can examine for yourself, and see if I am in fault, as Herod represents.

"Joseph buried Jesus in his own tomb. Whether he contemplated his resurrection or calculated to cut him another, I cannot tell. The day after he was buried one of the priests came to the praetorium and said they were apprehensive that his disciples intended to steal the body of Jesus and hide it, and then make it appear that he had risen from the dead, as he had foretold, and of which they were perfectly convinced. I sent him to the captain of the royal guard (Malcus) to tell him to take the Jewish soldiers, place as many around the sepulchre as were needed ; then if anything should happen they could blame themselves, and not the Romans.

"When the great excitement arose about the sepulchre being found empty, I felt a deeper solicitude than ever. I sent for Malcus, who told me he had placed his lieutenant, Ben Isham, with one hundred soldiers, around the sepulchre. He told me that Isham and the soldiers were very much alarmed at what had occurred there that morning. I sent for this man Isham, who related to me, as near as I can recollect, the following circumstances: He said that at about the beginning of the fourth watch they saw a soft and beautiful light over the sepulchre. He at first thought that the women had come to embalm the body of Jesus, as was their custom, but he could not see how they had gotten through the guards. While these thoughts were passing through his mind, behold, the whole place was lighted up, and there seemed to be crowds of the dead in their graveclothes. All seemed to be shouting and filled with ecstasy, while all around and above was the most beautiful music he had ever heard ; and the whole air seemed to be full of voices praising God. At this time there seemed to be a reeling and swimming of the earth, so that he turned so sick and faint that he could not stand on his feet. He said the earth seemed to swim from under him, and his senses left him, so that he knew not what did occur. I asked him in what condition he was when he came to himself. He said he was lying on the ground with his face down. I asked him if he could not have been mistaken as to the light. Was it not day that was coming in the East? He said at first he thought of that, but at a stone's cast it was exceedingly dark ; and then he remembered it was too early for day. I asked him if his dizziness might not have come from being wakened up and getting up too suddenly, as it sometimes had that effect. He said he was not, and had not been asleep all night, as the penalty was death for him to sleep on duty. He said he had let some of the soldiers sleep at a time. Some were asleep then. I asked him how long the scene lasted. He said he did not know, but he thought nearly an hour. He said it was hid by the light of day. I asked him if he went to the sepulchre after he had come to himself. He said no, because he was afraid; that just as soon as relief came they all went to their quarters. I asked him if he had been questioned by the priests. He said he had. They wanted him to say it was an earthquake, and that they were asleep, and offered him money to say that the disciples came and stole Jesus; but he saw no disciples ; he did not know that the body was gone until he was told. I asked him what was the private opinion of those priests he had conversed with. He said that some of them thought that Jesus was no man ; that he was not a human being ; that he was not the son of Mary ; that he was not the same that was said to be born of the virgin in Bethlehem ; that the same person had been on the earth before with Abraham and Lot, and at many times and places.

"It seems to me that, if the Jewish theory be true, these conclusions are correct, for they are in accord with this man's life, as is known and testified by both friends and foes, for the elements were no more in his hands than the clay in the hands of the potter. He could convert water into wine ; he could change death into life, disease into health ; he could calm the seas, still the storms, call up fish with a silver coin in its mouth. Now, I say, if he could do all these things, which he did, and many more, as the Jews all testify, and it was doing these things that created this enmity against him—he was not charged with criminal offenses, nor was he charged with violating any law, nor of wronging any individual in person, and all these facts are known to thousands, as well by his foes as by his friends—I am almost ready to say, as did Manulas at the cross, 'Truly this was the Son of God.'

"Now, noble Sovereign, this is as near the facts in the case as I can arrive at, and I have taken pains to make the statement very full, so that you may judge of my conduct upon the whole, as I hear that Antipater has said many hard things of me in this matter. With the promise of faithfulness and good wishes to my noble Sovereign,

"I am your most obedient servant,
"PONTIUS PILATE."

CHAPTER IX.

HEROD ANTIPATER'S DEFENCE BEFORE THE ROMAN SENATE IN REGARD TO HIS CONDUCT AT BETHLEHEM.

On a scroll in the library of the Vatican I find the following record, marked "Herod Antipater's Defence:"

"Noble Romans: In the case whereof I am accused, these Jews are of all people the most superstitious, and no more to be trusted than the Hindoos. They have taught themselves to believe in but one God, who dwells in another world, so they can neither see nor hear Him, nor in any way approach Him by their senses. They believe that He is unchangeable and unapproachable; that He can only manifest Himself through some angel or spirit, or some light, or the thunder, or any strange and uncommon phenomenon. Hence, they are so superstitious that they can be made to believe anything.

"In order that you may know what kind of people I have to deal with, I will give you some of their maxims: (1) When the sun shines they say their God smiles; (2) when it is cloudy they say He frowns; (3) when it thunders they say He is angry, and they hide themselves; (4) when it rains they say He weeps, and many other similar sayings. Now, my lords, you can see at once how far this people might be led, if they could be made to believe this strange God was at their head, and took up their cause.

"Now, as a foundation for all this foolishness, they have a book, and a set of men, called priests, who read and expound this book to them, and they will believe anything these priests tell them. To show how far they may be led, these priests tell them that some thousands of years ago one Moses died, and went to where this strange God dwelt. He was gone forty days, and when he came back he brought this book, which was written by this God for their government. Now, to prove the whole thing is a forgery, the book is wholly for the benefit of the priest. The poor have to work and toil continually, and pay half what they make, and sometimes almost starve to support the lazy priests and furnish them and their women with plenty of fine garments, and wine, and the best of food. The priests tell these poor Jews that this God requires them to bring the best calf, the best lamb, and the best flour and oil to the temple, to offer in sacrifice; and the priests and their party get all this for themselves. I often tell them, when they object to the Roman taxation, that they could keep up a thousand Caesars for much less than it costs to keep up their God and His priests.

"The leaders are always quarrelling and fighting among themselves, and dividing off in different sects.

Miracles are as common as poor physicians. The Essenes are noted for both. They prophesy, work miracles, see visions, and have dreams, and stand in reputation as quack doctors. They pretend to know all about angels, ghosts, and spirits ; they profess the art of managing ethereal citizens of transatmospheric regions. They live together in colonies, some of them are cenobitic and some are celibate communities. They maintain that all of them are priests and high priests ; therefore their daily baptisms as the priests on duty.

They wear the Levitical garments. Their tables are their altars, and their meals their only sacrifices. With this sanctimonious misanthropy, which is their highest virtue, they use the allegorical method of expounding the Scripture. While we think, and reason, and reflect, and use our faculties to obtain our ideas of duty, they shut their eyes and fold their hands, waiting to be endued with power from their God ; and when they get it, it proves to be all to their own advantage and interest, to the ruin of their fellow-citizens. The Sadducees are another party, equally absurd. They get their doctrine from Antigonus Sochaeus, who was President of the Sanhedrim. They reject all the traditions of the scribes and Pharisees. Then we find the *sopher*, or scribe. They are the writers and expounders of the law. The Pharisees (derived from *Pharash*, to separate) separate from all men on account of their sanctity. But it is useless to name all these sects, with their peculiar views, each differing from the other. They are all strict monotheists, yet they differ from each other more than the polytheists do.

"I have given this detailed description of the people and their various sects that the Senate may have an idea of the situation I am in. But if you could be here and see and associate with them as I do–to see them with all their sanctity of life, and then behold their treachery to each other ; see how they lie and steal the one from the other ; and then see how low and base are their priests– you would be much better qualified to judge of my actions.

"As to this great excitement at Bethlehem, three strange, fantastic-looking men called on my guards at the gate, and asked them where was the babe born that was to be King of the Jews. My guards told me of it, and I ordered the men to be brought into court. I asked them who they were. One of them said he was from Egypt. I asked what was their business. He said they were in search of the babe that was born to rule the Jews. I told them that I ruled the Jews under Augustus Caesar. But he said this babe would rule when I was gone. I told him not unless he was born under the purple. I asked him how he knew of this babe. He said they had all had a dream the same night about it. I told them that the devil played with our brains when we were asleep. He drew a parchment roll from his bosom, and read in the Hebrew language : 'Thou, Bethlehem, least among the kingdoms of the world, out of thee should come a man that should rule all people.' I asked him who wrote that. He said the God of heaven. I asked him where he got that parchment. He said it was the law of the covenant of the Jews. He also said a star had travelled before them all the way to Jerusalem. I told him his God was mistaken ; that Bethlehem was not a kingdom, neither was it the least in the kingdom of Judea. I told them that they were superstitious fanatics, and ordered them out of my presence.

"But the excitement grew until it became intense. I found nothing could control it. I called the Hillel court, which was the most learned body of talent in Jerusalem. They read out of their laws that Jesus was to be born of a virgin in Bethlehem; that he was to rule all nations, and all the kingdoms of the world were to be subject to him ; and that his kingdom should never end, but his appointees should continue this rule forever. I found this court just as sanguine as those strangers, and, in fact, it was in everybody's mouth ; I thought I could discover already a sort of deriding and mocking spirit among the lower classes in regard to the Roman authority. Now, it is my opinion that the scene that occurred at Bethlehem was nothing more than a meteor travelling through the air, or the rising vapor from the foot of the mountains out of the low, marshy ground, as is often the case. And as to the noise heard by Melker and those shepherd-boys, it was only the echo of the shepherds on the other side of the mountain calling the night-watch, or scaring away the wolves from their flocks.

"But although this was nothing but a phenomenon of nature, and the whole thing a delusion, it did not better the condition I was in. A man will contend for a false faith stronger than he will for a true one, from the fact that the truth defends itself, but a falsehood must be defended by its adherents: first, to prove it to themselves, and, secondly, that they may appear right in the estimation of their friends. But the fact is, this case is about as follows: The Roman taxation was cutting off the support of the priests, and they were smarting under it. Again, the double taxing—that is, the tithes to the priests and the tax to the Romans—was bearing heavily on the common people, so that they could not stand it, and the priests saw that one of them would have to go unpaid ; and, as they saw the Romans were the stronger, they wrote these things in the *Tosephta*, and read it daily in all their synagogues and temples, that the Jewish mind might be prepared for the event, knowing that they would magnify a mote into a mountain, when it came to anything outside of the common laws of nature, and knowing that if they could get the common people to believe in the things there would be no end to their fighting. And from all appearances the excitement was fast driving the people that way. It had already become a by-word with the children of Bethlehem and Jerusalem that the Jews had a new king, that neither Caesar nor Herod would reign any more, that they would have to pay no more taxes to keep up the Roman government. Such talk and sayings were common among the poorer classes of society.

So I saw an insurrection brewing fast, and nothing but a most bloody war as the consequence. Now, under these circumstances, what was I to do? In my honest judgment it was best to pluck the undeveloped flower in its bud, lest it should grow and strengthen, and finally burst, and shed its deadly poison over both nations, and impoverish and ruin them forever. My enemies can see I could have no malice toward the infants of Bethlehem. I took no delight in listening to the cries of innocent mothers. May all the gods forbid! No ; I saw nothing but an insurrection and a bloody war were our doom, and in this the overthrow and downfall, to some extent, of our nation.

"These are the grounds of my action in this matter. I am satisfied I did the best that could be done under the circumstances. As my motive was purely to do the best I could for my whole country, I hope you will so consider it, and I submit this statement for your consideration, promising faithfulness and submission to your judgment.

"HEROD ANTIPATER."

CHAPTER X.

HEROD ANTIPAS'S DEFENCE BEFORE THE ROMAN SENATE IN REGARD TO THE EXECUTION OF JOHN THE BAPTIST.

We found on the records of the Roman Senate Herod Antipas's defense respecting the various accusations preferred against him by different persons. In his defense there are some very important items regarding the Christian Church. The reader will notice that these events were recorded with no intention of establishing other facts. (1) The history of John the Baptist. (2) The history of Jesus Christ. (3) The killing of the children by his father at Bethlehem.

"TO TIBERIUS CAESAR AND THE SENATE OF ROME.

"*My Noble Lords, Greeting:* It is true, as my opponent asserts, that I was defeated in battle with Aretas, King of Arabia, but I was forced to fight when unprepared for the conflict. I either had to fight or have the country overrun by this wicked people. It is true I was defeated, but it was owing to the want of time and better preparation. Aretas came upon me without warning. Notwithstanding I was defeated his army was so crippled that he had to withdraw his forces from the field, and has not been able to rally them since. So our country was saved from the devastation of a foreign foe.

"I understand that the superstitious Jews say my defeat was for my wickedness in beheading John the Baptist. My understanding of the God of the Jews is, that He does not chastise the innocent for the crimes of the guilty. What did my actions have to do with the poor, suffering soldier? But if He had to punish all in order to reach me, then where is His almighty power they boast so much of ? I do not know whether their God was angry at me or not. There is one thing I know, the act was done with the holy intention of bringing the greatest amount of good to the greatest number of people; and if this is so, no court can gainsay it or condemn it.

"The facts in the case are about as follows: John the Baptist had set up a new mode of religion altogether different from the Jewish religion, teaching baptism instead of circumcision, which had been the belief and custom of the Jews in all ages past. According to their theory, God appeared to Abraham hundreds of years before, and told him with His own lips how and what to do to be saved ; and the Jews had lived according to this until it had become their nature, and all their forefathers had lived in this way. David, Solomon, Isaac, Jacob, and all the holy prophets had gone to heaven in this way of God's own appointment. Now, the question came to them, as they suggested it to me: Has God found that He was wrong ? Has His wisdom failed Him ? or has the unchangeable changed, and is He wavering in His purpose? Such would be the natural conclusion of a sensible man under the circumstances. Now, John the Baptist had no authority from God for what he was doing, as Abraham had. All he could say was, 'He that sent me to baptize is true;' and he cannot tell who he was. Then his going into the wilderness: God had ordered Solomon to build the finest temple that was ever built in the world, and made promises that whosoever came to that house with his offerings his prayers should be heard and answered. This temple had been the place of their meeting for hundreds of years, for the Jews think this temple the next place to heaven.

"Now see the difference:

"1st. John has no authorized authority.

"2d. He changes God's place of worship.

"3d. He changes the doctrines.

"4th. He changes the mode of application.

"Now, the idea of Gamaliel was that John wanted to be some great man; hence, he took this mode of eccentric life to establish it. And there is nothing better qualified than the course he took to make an impression upon the ignorant and unlearned—to go away out into the wilderness by himself, get a few friends from Jerusalem to go out and hear him, and come back and tell of the great wonders which they had seen in the wilderness. Then John's appearance—his long, uncombed hair and beard, his fantastic clothing, and his food, nothing but bugs and beans—such a course and such a character are well qualified to lead the illiterate astray. These troubles on the Jewish mind were very heavy, and gave such men as Hilderium, Shammai, Hillel, and others great concern. And no wonder, for in their judgment it was vacating the temple of religious worship; it was blocking the road to heaven, and driving the poor and unsuspecting to ruin, as well as destroying the whole nation. So it was, by their request, as so ordered, that it was better to execute one to save the many from a worse fate. And this is the true reason for the deed, and not to please the whim of a dancing-girl, as you have heard. Now, my lords, if this is not satisfactory, I would ask my accuser, Caius, to write to any of the learned Jews, and learn if my statement is not correct.

"As to Agrippa's accusing me of having arms for seventy thousand soldiers, it is correct; but they were left me by my father, Herod the Great. And as they were needed to defend the province, and I did not know it was necessary to report them, I never thought of keeping them secret. But as to my being in league with Sejonius, I appeal to the virtue of my conduct, and demand investigation.

"As to what Pontius Pilate says in regard to my cowardice and disobedience in the case of Jesus of Nazareth, I will say in my own defence: I was informed by all the Jews that this was the same Jesus that my father aimed to destroy in his infancy; for I have it in my father's private writings and accounts of his life, showing that when the report was circulated of three men inquiring where was he that was born King of the Jews, he called together the Hillel and Shammai schools, and demanded the reading of the sacred scrolls; that it was decided he was to be born in Bethlehem of Judea, as read and interpreted that night by Hillel. So when my father learned that there was a birth of a male child in Bethlehem under very strange circumstances, and he could not learn who nor where the child was, he sent and had the male children slain that were near his age. Afterward he learned that his mother had taken him and fled into the wilderness. For this attempt to uphold the Roman authority in the land of Judea the world has not ceased to curse him to this day; and yet the Caesars have done a thousand worse things, and done them a thousand times, and it was all well. Just think how many lives have been lost to save the Roman Empire; while those infants were only removed in their innocence from the evil to come. The proper way to judge of action is to let the actor judge, or the one with whom the action terminates. If this should be done, and there is a life of happiness beyond this for innocence to dwell in, those infants as well as the Rachels should be thankful to my father for the change. Again, my lords, Pilate is a higher officer than I; and you know in our law the lower court always has the right to appeal to the higher. As to Pilate's saying that Jesus was a Galilean, he is mistaken. Jesus was born in Bethlehem of Judea, as the records show. And as to his citizenship, he had none. He wandered about from place to place having no home, making his abode principally with the poor. He was a wild fanatic, who had taken up the doctrines of John (but not his baptism) and was quite an enthusiast. He had learned soothsaying, while in Egypt, to perfection. I tried to get him to perform some miracle while in my court, but he was too sharp to be caught in a trap; like all necromancers, he was afraid to show off before the intelligent. From what I could learn he had reprimanded some of the rich Jews for their meanness and his reproaches were not out of the way, from what I heard they would have been much better men if they had practised what he preached.

"So this is my defense. I submit it for your consideration, praying for clemency.
"HEROD ANTIPAS."

CHAPTER XI

THE HILLEL LETTERS REGARDING GOD'S PROVIDENCE TO THE JEWS, BY HILLEL THE THIRD.

[The following letters were translated and sent to me after my return home–MAHAN.]

First Letter.

"To the noble and persecuted sons of my Father, God, who is too wise to err in His judgment, and too mighty to let His kingdom suffer or His children to be persecuted beyond what is good for them :

Beholding our desolate condition, we must know there is a good reason somewhere. From our former history, and the dealings of God with our forefathers, it is evident that it is not because He is neglectful of the interests of His children. It must be on our own account.

"In directing your thoughts to these subjects, it is needful to call your attention to the acts of God in the history of the world. By this we may learn the cause of our present condition. When He was dissatisfied with the wicked world His eyes rested on one good man, Noah. Now, it is useless for us to begin a controversy as to how Noah became good. That is nothing to us. The great question for us is, Are we good? and if not, why are we wicked? No doubt this is the reason we are forsaken. If we could not help our being wicked, then we are persecuted wrongfully. But it was the goodness of Noah that preserved his life, and made him a great and happy man;

man; while it was wickedness that caused all the rest of the world to be drowned.

"Then follow along the line to Abraham. God found him faithful, and on this account He made him the father of all that are faithful and good, And so with hundreds of others that I could name in our former history. I would ask all the Jews in their dispersed condition to read the history of our race and see the dealings of God to the good, and His judgments upon the evil.

"Now, God makes selections of certain individuals to relieve others. These chosen ones may not be good, but those for whom they are selected must be good, or they can receive no favor from God.

Look at Moses. He was an infant. He could neither be good nor bad, because he was at that time powerless. But Israel was good, and it was by reason of Israel's goodness that Moses was selected. Hence, from this babe in the basket we find the long chain of displays of God's mighty works in saving and defending and comforting the good, simply and alone because they were good ; and this is the only reason why God has ever bestowed special favors on anyone, just because He is good, and I am sure this is all that is necessary to justify Him in His dealings with the sons of men. If He creates men, and gives them all necessary power and opportunities to be good and they refuse, then they are to blame, and not He. This is the reason He condemned the world to a flood. This is the reason the Egyptians were drowned. This is the reason the Sodomites were burned. This is the reason the Canaanites were destroyed. This is the reason we were sold into Babylon. And oh ! for a master spirit to rise up, as did Samuel to Saul, to tell us the reason we are again forsaken and cast away; why is it that our city and the holy temple are forsaken and desolate? Why is it that God fights no more battles for Israel? Why is it that we have no leader that it would be safe for the people to follow? Why is it that Israel is turned against herself, that every evil bird is permitted to pluck her, and her best friends are turned to be her enemies? Why is it that Josephus sold Galilee to the Romans? Why is it that the sanctifying of the Spirit is withdrawn? Why is it that the Urim and the Thummim in the temple have not changed the color of its stones in thirty years? Why is it that the light of the threshold in the temple has ceased to burn? And why is it that the Jews have lost the feeling of brotherhood, and fight each other like beasts of hell until God has given us over, and permitted the Romans to, devour our heritage, to burn our city, to destroy our beloved temple, and drench it with the blood of its devotees?

"I know that many of my brethren, more particularly the priests, will bring grave charges against the ministration and, of course, indirectly impeach God; but it may be, my brethren, we mistake God's designs in all this thing. And may we not be equally mistaken in regard to our desert or our demerit in His dealing with us? We know that the guilty party is apt to think the law is too severe; but we never think so when others are to suffer, and especially if we are the party against whom the criminal has offended and done wrong.

"When a Jew becomes mean and wicked and violates the Jewish law and injures us personally, then we propose to stone him until he is dead, if his actions have been such to deserve such a sentence; and we are equally guilty if we in any way try to screen the criminal from suffering the just penalty of the law. Now let us, as honest Jews, look in our own natures and examine our actions in the light of God's holy revelation, and see if our present condition is not deserving on our part; and if we find that it is we who have forsaken God, instead of His having forsaken us, then let us do as our fathers did in Egypt; do as our fathers did in Babylon. They hung their harps ; they clothed themselves in sackcloth and ashes; they mourned as do the dove and the pelican. So did they seek rest until the Lord God Jehovah was moved with compassion. They not only ceased to act wickedly, but they showed by their regrets and acknowledgment that they would act differently in the future ; and God had compassion on them, and moved the heart of their wicked king to pity them, that they might return and rebuild their temple. These were the ways in which they conducted themselves ; and look at the results that followed. now these things were for their own good, and they were recorded that we might learn what to do, provided we should be brought into the same condition.

"Now, I wish my Jewish brethren to understand that I am not a follower of this Nazarene that has created so much strife among the people, neither do I indorse his new doctrines; yet I think it would be well for us not to be too hasty in forming our conclusions on this or any other subject. I heard Peter preach the other day, and as he and John came out of the temple there was a man that had been lying around at the gates and public crossings for years. He was unable to walk, having no soundness in his feet and ankle-bones. As they were passing him he asked them for help. Peter said he had nothing to give, but, said he, 'In the name of Jesus the Son of God, I say unto thee, rise up and walk ;' and the man sprang to his feet, seemingly perfectly sound, and commenced praising God at the top of his voice, which caused a great commotion among the people, and the police came and took Peter and John to prison as peace-breakers. I thought I never saw such an outrage. It is right to arrest men for doing evil, but to arrest and imprison men for doing good is something I cannot comprehend. This has been the fault of us Jews in all time. No odds what good was done, if it was not done just as the priest thought it ought to be done, it was wrong. When I saw the act of Peter toward the helpless man, I said to myself, 'There is the power of Moses ; there is the power of Jehovah manifest in human flesh; there is the power needed by us Jews to reinstate the king born of heaven ; this is the power that has followed the Jews in times past, and the only distinguishing mark that makes us different from the other nations of the earth. This was the peculiar power of Jesus of Nazareth ; and because he did not work according to Jewish rule they condemned him to die. It was not because his works were not good works, but because he did not do them according to Jewish custom.'

"I was forcibly struck with Peter's sermon, He said: 'There was a rich man who had one son. This son had been trying for a long time to build him a house. He was homeless and exposed to many dangers and trouble for the want of a house, until he was almost exhausted and was ready to perish. And his father had compassion on his son and built him a house, with everything needful for the necessities and comforts of his child. And when it was finished he went and brought his son to see it. And

And his son was delighted, and said it was much better than he could have built himself. And his father said, "Son, I love you. I give you this house. Will you accept it?" "With all my heart, dear, father, with grateful acknowledgments." Now,' Peter said, 'here is the picture of the world which has been working, struggling, and striving for ties to build them a home for the soul of man. They have worked by the laws of men, by building fine temples, by offering sacrifices, by paying tithes to the Lord, by walking hundreds of miles to the temple barefooted and bareheaded, by keeping holy days and festivals, and all to no purpose. The soul has become wearied out of patience, and still no rest, until man has become dissatisfied not only with himself, but with his God and his service. And while in this despairing condition God our Father comes in the person of Jesus, whom the Jews crucified and in his death he prepared a house of rest, and now proposes to his children to accept what he has done for them, and stop working and worrying to try to fit themselves for a higher station and a happier life.' And Peter asked, 'Who will accept?'

"Again Peter said : 'This house was beautiful to look at, and was in every way suited to the son, yet he could not enjoy it from the fact that it had no furniture. So the son went to work and toiled and labored trying to make furniture to suit himself. But notwithstanding he could not get a piece that would last. And it soon became useless because it did not suit him. Then the father went to work and made all manner of ware, and presented it to his son. Every piece fitted the place and suited the purpose for which it was made, so that the son was well pleased. And the father said : "All this will I give you, my son, because I love you. Will you accept?" The son said, "With all my heart, dear father; this pleases me better than if I had had the power to make it myself," Now,' said Peter, 'this is what God has done for the world. Instead of purifying ourselves by washing, by fasting, by prayers, by penitence, and by all the works of the law, God has given us a purity that will last forever, that will suit us and will please Him.'

"Again said Peter: 'This son was all ragged. His clothes were worn threadbare in trying to build and fit him a house, and he was ashamed. So he went to work to try to clothe himself ; and the harder he worked the less success rewarded him. And after he had worked hard, his father went to work and wove him a seamless robe, and presented it to his son, and said, "My son, I love you, and I have prepared a white robe; will you accept it?" "With many thanks, dear father," said the son. "Oh, how beautiful it is! How snowy white! How well it fits me ! Oh ! father, I never can feel grateful enough. I thought thou wast angry and hated me, because I was poor and homeless and miserable and ragged ; but if thou didst love me in my misery, I know thou canst love me now, and will delight to make thy abode with me forevermore. Oh ! father, I don't know how to show my gratitude to thee." The son was delighted with the change, while the father was equally delighted with the son, and they both rejoiced. And the father said to the son: "I delight to dwell with my children when they live in a manner that is suited to my taste ; and, of course, this suits me, from the fact it is all my own work. Only be content, and do not soil thy robe, for it is so white and clean, a very little mixing with dirt and filth will so contaminate it, it will not be fit to be seen. And as long as you keep it unspotted from the world it will distinguish you from the world and make you a welcome visitor into the company of all that are dressed in the same robe ; for this is merely the outward showing of the principles that live within; which principles are only developed by the outward appearance. And even it will be admired by those who may reject it; yet inwardly they must respect it. Though they may covet it, and raise the spirit of persecution against you, it is not because they dislike you, but because they are not like you ; and this is the cause of envy everywhere." This,' said Peter, 'is the way God our Father has treated us spiritually. He has prepared us a holy habitation, where our immortal souls can live and be happy through all eternity, and then has given us the Holy Spirit, the same that Jesus promised and the same that fell on the people the other day. This spirit renews and begets within us holy desires to love God and to serve Him by obeying all His commands and doing honor to His name. And this same spirit begets within us a holy desire to see all men embrace the offering of this good and noble Father, that they may be happy now and happy forever, more so after death than before ; for it is the dread of meeting an interminable doom for our sins that makes our lives intolerable. Oh!' said Peter, 'behold the riches offered on terms so easy by our Father. All we need is to accept. Who will accept ?' And there were two or three hundred who cried out, 'We will;' and then followed a mighty rising up and rejoicing, all of which made a very strong impression on my mind.

"I am going to make a most thorough examination

into these things to see if they are so–if God has provided an easier and a better way to save the souls of men than the Jewish economy. I feel that the subject is worth looking into ; for of long time it has seemed to me (and my father saw and spoke of the same) that the ways of God's service were exacting, and apt to make men become indifferent, and almost to look on God as a haughty tyrant ; while Peter's illustration shows Him in such a lovely light it makes me love Him."

Second Letter.

After having viewed our present condition, it may be well for us to look back and review our former history, and get a knowledge of the state of the world in former times. If we look at the world from the pages of Ezra, Nehemiah, and Haggai, the last of God's prophets upon earth, we will see a period of nearly five hundred years to the present, during which time the world underwent greater changes than ever before. We will see our nation returning from a seventy years' captivity, recommencing their national existence after having been overrun and absorbed in the first great monarchy that swept over the earth. Our acquaintance with the rest of the world was very limited, extending only to the Chaldeans, the Phoenicians, the Egyptians, and a few unimportant tribes. Our ideas seem to have been likewise limited, extending but little beyond the principles of the Mosaic religion, which had been promulgated about fifteen hundred years before.

"I am informed that the accusation against Jesus was written over him as he hung upon the cross, in Hebrew,

Greek, and Latin. Whence came these dialects? When the prophets closed their writings (which was nearly five hundred years ago), the Greek was scarcely a written language, confined to a small part of Europe, and Rome, from which the Latin language came, was a straggling village on the banks of the Tiber. During this whole period, in which nations and monarchies were born, flourished, and decayed (showing clearly a providential preparation), the intermingling of the various languages indicates preparation for some great event, and to my mind makes the juncture most opportune for the introduction of a universal religion. That is, if I understand it aright, God has arranged the position and the existence of the several nations of the earth in such a manner as to promote the recognition, the establishment, and the propagation of true religion, the knowledge and worship of the true God.

"Whatever knowledge may have been imparted to our ancestors, or however long it may have lasted, certain it is that at the time of Abraham the nations generally had fallen into idolatry. To him God was pleased to make himself known, and to promise that of him He would make a great nation, and in him and his seed all the nations of the earth should be blessed. That is, through him and his posterity he would impart the greatest possible good, the knowledge of the true God. To accomplish this purpose God selected the spot in which he and his posterity were to be placed ; and no spot on earth could have been better suited for the purpose. The land of Canaan, afterward called Judea, afterward called Palestine, a tract of country situated about midway between the three great divisions of the earth—Asia, Africa, and Europe—on the great highway of nations, in the very path of conquest, commerce, and travel, was equally accessible to all parts of the then known world.

"But those circumstances which afterward made Judea so favorably located as the radiating point of the true faith did not exist in the time of Abraham. There was neither conquest nor commerce nor travel. The world was overrun by wandering tribes, scarcely having boundaries or fixed habitations. Chaldea, the cradle of the human race, and Egypt, the birthplace of human learning and the arts, were the only nations of consequence at that time. It is not probable that any such thing as alphabetic writing existed ; for we read that Abraham took no other evidence of the purchase which he made of a burying-place for his family than living witnesses of the bargain. At that period, therefore, divine communication must have been confined to individuals. The fulness of time had not yet come even for that partial revelation which was made by Moses. There was no mode by which it could be recorded and preserved. The invention of writing was necessary to prepare the world for it. That invention took place some time within the five hundred years which elapsed between Abraham and Moses.

"Into Egypt, the mother of the arts, the posterity of Abraham were sent as if to school, not in divine things (for in the knowledge of them the shepherds of Canaan as far exceeded the refined Egyptians as light exceeds darkness), but in the knowledge of those things by which life is rendered comfortable. When they had become sufficiently numerous to take possession of the destined territory, a leader was raised up for that especial purpose–Moses, the child of a slave, his life exposed in infancy in a frail cradle of rushes upon the waters, yet destined to be the mightiest agent in the affairs of men that the Almighty had ever employed on earth. Who can but admire the wisdom of Divine Providence in the education of this great founder of nations, this prophet of divine truth, this enlightener of the world? Who can apprehend the glorious position which he holds in the world's history ? What a distinction to have framed the constitution of a nation which lasted fifteen hundred years, and stamped a people with the marks of nationality which time itself has not obliterated ! To have written a book which has been read with interest and ardor by passing ages and growing millions of the human race ! To impart to nations and continents the saving knowledge of the one true God ! What a glory to have laid by one sentence the foundation of true religion in so many millions of minds: 'In the beginning God created the heavens and the earth.'

"The more I contemplate the mission of Moses, the higher he rises in moral sublimity in my estimation. If I contemplate him during the forty years of his sojourn in the wilderness, he is the only depository of the true religion on earth, with the exception of the tribe he led. The whole world was sunk in the debasement of idolatry. What a noble use did the Almighty make of the recent invention of man's ingenuity, the invention of letters, to engrave upon stone his awful testimony against the great, fundamental, and all-polluting sin of the world, the worship of idols: 'Thou shalt have no other Gods before me; thou shalt not make unto thee any graven image, or the likeness of anything that is in the heaven above or in the earth beneath; thou shalt not bow down thyself to them nor serve them.' To realize and carry out this one thing was the purpose in separating the Jews from the rest of the world ; and with all the seals and signs, and God's special judgments, it took fourteen hundred years to do it, so prone are we to worship the things that are seen, instead of the unseen. And this is one of the great troubles at the present day. This is one reason of our desolation. We thought too much of our holy city and temple; but if this was our sin, what might we expect from men in the state of ignorance in the days of Moses? Oh, brethren, let us ask ourselves, are we not more inclined to worship the created things than we are to worship Him who created them ? Look at this people I am speaking of. Forty days had not elapsed from the utterance from Sinai of this fundamental precept, 'Thou shalt have no, other Gods before me,' when the very people to whom this command was given made for themselves a golden calf, after the manner of the idolatrous Egyptians, and danced before it with great joy. To secure this one grand and fundamental point (that is, the worship of the only living and true God), the whole Mosaic economy was modelled. For this purpose we were forbidden to marry foreigners; for this purpose our sacrifices were all to be offered in one place, and by one family of priests, lest we should wander away and become corrupt by association with idolaters. For this purpose we were forbidden certain kinds of food, such as were offered in sacrifices to heathen deities. We were not to be present at idolatrous feasts, nor to become accustomed to those moral abominations with which heathen worship was invariably accompanied. More effectually to secure this point, Divine Providence so arranged it that our national existence and prosperity depended on our fidelity to the great purpose for which we were set apart. Whenever we worshipped the true God and obeyed His laws, temporal prosperity was the natural consequence; then were union and peace and industry and prosperity. But whenever we forsook God and worshipped idols, a corresponding degeneracy of morals and makers took place. This was followed by discord, weakness, poverty, and subjection to foreign nations.

"But the event which exerted the most decisive influence upon the national existence of us Jews was the erection of Solomon's temple at Jerusalem. Before that time our sacred rites had been conducted in a very humble manner. Our sacred utensils had no better covering than a tent. Often they were in private custody; and once the sacred ark itself, which contained the heaven-derived charter of our national existence, was taken captive and remained for months in the country of the Philistines. That ark for nearly four hundred years was almost the only bond of our national union, the only object around which gathered our national reverence; and, although in our younger years we were apt to regard that ark and its contents with a childish curiosity, in after years we came to look upon it as an object of higher significance. It is the written testimony of God against idolatry. It contains the fundamental articles of our nation's constitution.

It is a charter from God for a nation's establishment and independence. It is a declaration of principles, which was borne before us like a banner, proclaiming to the world for what we were to live, for what we were to fight, for what we were to die. It was our confession of faith, which we upheld before the world as sacred, true, and vital to the best interest of humanity, and the only hope of our final success. Once abandon this and we are lost, disgraced, fallen forever. On the tables in that ark were written: 'Thou shalt have no other Gods before me;' and, 'Thou shalt not make any graven image, nor the likeness of anything ; thou shalt not bow down to anything to serve them.' There it remains from age to age as the memorial of the purpose of our national existence; and how mightily has it worked in the earth !

"There is an incident related by the sacred historian which may seem symbolical of the mission of the whole dispensation which that sacred enclosure contained. It is the fifth section of Samuel : 'And the Philistines took the ark and brought it from Ebenezer to Ashdod. When the Philistines took the ark of God, they brought it into the house of Dagon; and when they of Ashdod arose early on the morrow, behold, Dagon was fallen upon his face to the earth before the ark of the Lord, and they took Dagon and set him in his place again; and when they rose early on the morrow morning, behold, Dagon was fallen to his face to the ground again before the ark of the Lord, and the head of Dagon and the palms of his hands were cut off upon the threshold: only the stump of Dagon was left unto him.'

"So is all idolatry destined to fall before the word of the Almighty. So has our Dagon fallen—and oh ! what a dreadful fall it is to us Israelites. Let me tell you what was achieved in the Temple of Azotus was gradually accomplished throughout the land of Israel. Many times has Dagon been set up in his place again ; many times has idolatry been revived ; the ark of God has been in the hands of the enemy (it is there now at this time), and the true religion about to be extinguished, when the Almighty interposed to vindicate His honor and reestablish His worship, and at last obtained a triumph by the very means which at first threatened to overthrow it forever.

"I have said that the objects of our national existence were greatly promoted by the building of the temple at Jerusalem. It was a splendid edifice, calculated to awaken the curiosity, to attract the attention, and command the respect of the world. It furnished a place of appropriate convenience, beauty, and dignity for the celebration of our daily sacrifices and our national rites. It made more interesting our three yearly festivals when all the males were obliged to present themselves before God. It gave us what we all need at this time–a fixture to our religion, a local habitation to our religious applications and associations. It connected the sentiment of religion with another no less strong–that of patriotism– and enlisted them both in the maintenance and defence of the national institutions of Moses ; and it also led to the formation of a national literature which gave expression to these two most powerful sentiments of the human heart, and thus operated to call forth and strengthen them in each succeeding generation.

'Still the Mosaic institutions, assisted by the magnificence of the temple service, failed to extirpate entirely the propensity to idolatry. Occasionally it sprang up and overspread the country, till at last the

Almighty saw fit to suffer that temple to be overthrown, His people to be carried into captivity, and His worship to be suspended for seventy years ; and His judgments accomplished what His mercies could not do. The very measure of Divine severity which at first sight threatened to sweep the worship of the true God from the face of the earth, and give up the world to the interminable dominion of idolatry, was the means of establishing it on a firmer basis than ever. Although Jerusalem was overthrown and the temple razed to its foundation, the Jews carried the true Jerusalem in their hearts. And so it is to-day. Although our holy city is no more, and although we are dispersed and many of us sold into slavery, yet the holy temple of our God lives and will continue to live in our hearts forever. Wherever we go, whether in the splendid cities of the East, or amid the fascinations of Egypt, or the tents of the wandering shepherds, still our affections will be in the holy land, and, like Daniel, we will turn our faces toward the land where our fathers worshipped the God of heaven.

"Nehemiah, when serving in the courts of princes, lamented when he heard that the walls of Jerusalem were thrown down. There in slavery, our fathers had time to reflect upon the cause of their calamities; there they read in the Book of Moses, which was the companion of their exile, the awful curses He had threatened them if they forsook the worship of the true God, and felt them to be fulfilled in themselves ; there they read the prophecy which had been written by Moses more than a thousand years before in the book, iii., section 22 : 'If thou wilt not observe to do all the words of this law that are written in this book, that thou mayest fear this glorious and fearful name, the Lord thy God, the Lord will scatter thee among all people, from one end of the earth to the other, and among these nations thou shalt find no ease, neither shall the sole of thy foot have rest; but the Lord will give thee then a trembling heart and failing eyes, and sorrow of mind, and thy life shall hang in doubt before thee: and thou shalt fear night and day, and have no assurance of thy life. In the morning thou shalt say, Would God it were evening, and at even thou shalt say, Would God it were morning! for the fear of thine heart wherewith thou shalt fear, and for the sight of thine eyes which thou shalt see.' Thus were our fathers smitten to the heart by the fulfilment of such awful threatenings. All propensity to idolatry was forever cured. Never after this period could the allurements of pleasure or the threats of pain, neither dens of wild beasts nor the fiery furnace, neither instant death nor lingering torture, ever induce them to offer sacrifice to idol gods. This same Providence which had scattered them in foreign lands, now restored them to their own. Their temple was rebuilt, the daily sacrifice was resumed and was never intermitted, with the exception of about three years under Antiochus Epiphanes.

"But now let us look at our present state, and see how we, their children, have fallen : The ark once more is taken from us; Jerusalem is in ruins, trodden by the foot of the Gentiles ; ruin has driven her ploughshare through the crumbling walls, and we are scattered to mix and mingle among all nations."

Third Letter.

"As all the nations of the earth lacked the knowledge of the true God except us Jews, it devolved on us as a nation to extend this knowledge to all the world, which was brought about by the following plan : First, by the universal diffusion of the Greek language, and, secondly, by the conquest of the world by the Romans. Another cause almost as essential was the scattering of our nation among all nations of the earth, for narrowness and bigotry had almost made us a barren tree as to any general good for the world. So ancient were our habits and fixed our customs that spiritual life was almost extinct ; therefore it was necessary for us even to learn a new language, that the knowledge of the true God might be infused into a new medium, and thus be spread from land to land. It was necessary that the true medicine of life should be dissolved in an element which flowed on every shore and in every stream that all men might taste thereof and be saved. It was necessary, too, that a foreign language should be forced upon us ; for nothing but conquest and constraint, nothing but this, could overcome our bitter prejudices. It will be the object of this letter to show how this was brought about.

"The great designs of God were advanced by our misfortunes as well as by our prosperity, and in God's purpose of preparing the world for the advent of a higher life and greater attainment in godliness, each event had a ripening tendency. Whether we worshipped in Jerusalem in peace or wept by the rivers of Babylon, everywhere and under all circumstances we taught a knowledge of the true God ; and everywhere our nation has cherished the hope of triumph in the expectation of a coming Messiah. The first great empire to which Judea fell a prey was the Babylonian. Jerusalem was destroyed by Nebuchadnezzar five hundred and fifty-seven years ago ; and the remnant of the people was carried to Babylon and the neighboring countries, whither the main body had been removed eighteen years before. The glimpses of those times and countries are very short, but enough is given us to see that the residence of our fathers in those countries was not without effect.

"It is impossible to put out the light of a Jew's eye, or to extinguish the fire that burns in his heart ; and the life of our fathers made lasting effects both on the people they were with and themselves also. One person especially adorned that dark period of God's exiled Church. The prophet, Daniel, gives us almost the only sight we get of mighty Babylon ; his writings furnish us with a number of great truths. He passes before us from youthful beauty to extreme age. We see him rising, like Joseph, by early wisdom, piety, and integrity, from slavery, to be the chief minister of State, and it is altogether probable that it was through him that Cyrus was prompted to restore our people to our holy land again. The edict was issued in the first year of his reign, immediately after the capture of Babylon, which Daniel had foretold by interpreting the writing on the wall.

"But the restoration of our nation, an event so wonderful and strange in the history of the world, though properly attributed to the providence of God, was brought about by means more circuitous than is generally supposed. Fifty or a hundred thousand Jews did not live in Babylonia, Media, and Persia seventy years–making such a singularly religious impression—for nothing. Our people appear to have been treated with much more respect among these oriental nations than in the western world. The reason of this, probably, was that the Persians, like the Arabians, their neighbors, had not forsaken the patriarchal religion or sunk into such gross and degrading idolatry as those nations which had wandered farthest from the paternal hearthstone of the human race.

It is in this period of our nation's sojourn in the East that the famous reformer, Zoroaster, appeared. I look upon him as the second Moses, though without inspiration ; but, availing himself of the light of the true revelation, he attempted not to introduce a new religion, but to refine, purify, and build up the religion of his country by introducing into it the most important principles of the true faith, and thus, with a mixture of base and noble motives, to benefit his country, and reflect glory on himself. The secret of his success was, he taught the theology of Moses, and his theology was so simple and sublime, and so consonant at the same time with the best conceptions of mankind that it clothed this impostor with the veneration of his countrymen, and sanctified even his crimes and follies. It was from Moses that Zoroaster derived the idea of one living God, the maker of heaven and earth ; but he corrupted this pure doctrine by making two subordinate gods, the authors respectively of good and evil. From Moses he received an utter abhorrence of all images and of the temples in which they were worshipped, but he introduced, in connection with the true faith, the doctrine of evil spirits dividing the government of the universe. So it happened that there was not only an impress of the religion of our fathers upon that of the Persians, but a reaction of the Persian religion upon that of our nation.

"The Jews, as would appear from the book of Tobit, first learned in their captivity those ideas of the agency of evil spirits in the world, of which we find traces in all their histories. Cyrus was a Persian, and in all probability had been instructed in the doctrines of Zoroaster, a combination, as we have seen, of Judaism and the ancient Persian religion ; hence his extraordinary partiality for the Jews is explained, and his zeal in rebuilding the only temple on earth which was dedicated in his name to the God of heaven, and was free from the all-pervading and polluting sin of idol-worship.

"But the influence of Zoroaster did not end here. The successors of Cyrus were educated in his religion. The priests and teachers of his religion were called Magi, and exerted a powerful influence in the State. Darius Hystaspes, son-in-law and successor of Cyrus, warmly espoused the religion of the Persian philosopher, and when Zoroaster was slain by an eruption of the Scythians, he amply avenged his death, and rebuilt the fine temples which the Scythians had destroyed, especially, and with more splendor than before, the one in which Zoroaster ministered. It was this enmity to idolatry, thus derived through Zoroaster from Moses, which was the only redeeming principle that the Persian monarchs showed in all their extensive conquests. Cambyses, the son of Cyrus, madman and tyrant as he was, derives a sort of dignity from his zeal against idolatry. His indignation at seeing the Egyptians worship a living brute does honor at least to his Persian education, though in other respects he was a cruel and detestable tyrant. When Darius and Xerxes marched their mighty armies into Europe, the only idea which these vast expeditions were intended to carry out, that can excite the least sympathy in the mind of a Jew, was the destruction of idolatry, which they everywhere threatened and attempted to realize. Thus it is that the mind governs at last. The Persian kings, with their vast armies, bearing war and subjugation to remotest lands, were only realizing ideas which had been matured by Zoroaster in his cave, and which he in turn had derived from Moses. "Thus through our exiled fathers the hand became the executive of the brain to establish the worship of the true God, and in the revolution of the wheels of nature, as seen by Ezekiel, the soldier is the machine of the thinker and armies are assembled and battles fought to carry out a few ideas with which men of letters have filled the mind of a nation, and scholars and sages, prophets and impostors, good men and bad men, kings and generals, armies and revolutions, are all equally used to accomplish the purposes of that eternal Mind, who sitteth supreme over all, which we as the only nation known on earth recognize as Divine Providence.

"The ambition of Cyrus and his successors, though in a manner which they did not anticipate, was the means made use of by our Father of introducing among the enslaved and ignorant multitude of the East the civilization, the arts, and the learning which Greece, with her wonderful genius, had matured. Cyrus, whose sudden irruption into Babylon terminated Belshazzar's feast and fulfilled so terribly the writing on the wall, had already extended the Persian Empire over the greater part of Asia Minor. Belshazzar, the last king over Babylon, attempted to strengthen himself against the growing power of the Persians, by forming an alliance with Croesus, King of Lydia, so famous for his riches. This monarch, made arrogant by his great wealth and the command of an army of nearly half a million, resolved to encounter the Persian power, but lately become formidable. To make assurance doubly sure, he sent to inquire of the Oracle at Delphi in Greece, and received for answer: 'If Croesus pass the Holys,' the boundary between Lydia and Persia, 'he shall destroy a great empire.' He went, and found that empire was his own. He was defeated by Cyrus, and his whole kingdom came into the hands of the conqueror five hundred and forty years ago. This conquest brought the Persians in collision with the Greeks, and was the cause of those wars which were waged with such bitterness for generations between the two nations, and finally resulted in the destruction of the Persian monarchy. The Greeks, though natives of Europe, had planted many colonies on the Asiatic coast. These colonies, though infinitely superior to the effeminate and luxurious Asiatics in every physical, intellectual, and moral attribute, were altogether unable to resist the overwhelming weight of an empire which reached from Ethiopia to the Caspian Sea, and from the Indus to the Bosphorus. They were obliged to submit, like the rest, and pay an annual tribute to their conquerors, no less to the humiliation and annoyance of the mother-country than themselves. The yoke at length became so oppressive that they resolved to throw it off. To effect this they applied to Athens and Sparta for aid. Receiving assistance from these most considerable states of Greece, they rebelled, marched to Sardis, took it, and accidentally set the city on fire, by which it was totally consumed. The loss of this city, the richest in Asia Minor, exasperated Darius, King of Persia, to the highest degree, and kindled in his breast such a flame of resentment that he resolved upon revenge. Lest in his multifarious affairs he should forget the offenders, he appointed officers whose duty it was each day to repeat to him as he dined, 'Sir, remember the Athenians.' Resolved to punish these presumptuous republics which had dared to brave the whole power of the Persian Empire, he collected a fleet and army sufficient, as he supposed, to crush so small a country at one blow. After an ineffectual attempt to reach Greece by this circuitous route of Thrace and Macedonia, a second armament was fitted out, of the flower of that army which had borne conquest on their banners from the Euphrates to the Nile, and transported by sea directly toward the little republic of Athens, able then to send into the field but from ten to fifteen thousand men. The Athenians met and vanquished them on the plain of Marathon, leaving six thousand dead on the field. Thus ended the first attempt of Persian despotism upon the liberties of Greece. This may be said to be the first demonstration that was ever given to the world of the benefits of free government. A few ages of absolute political liberty had trained up a race of men such as had never been seen before. Intelligence combined with physical force, thorough discipline, and an enthusiastic love of country, for the first time were brought to contend hand to hand with the pampered sons of Eastern luxury and the spiritless automata of a despotic government. The result was what it will ever be. The Orientals fell like grass before the swords of the free. But this defeat, so far from discouraging the conqueror of the Indies, only roused him to mightier efforts. He immediately resolved on invading Greece with a larger army than before ; but in the midst of his preparations he fell before a mightier conqueror, and left the inheritance of his kingdom and his revenge to his son, Xerxes, who was destined still further to add to the glory of Greece, though it would seem that this son could have seen, in the providence of God, that man with men combined could not contend with the Almighty. But this youth, succeeding to the mightiest monarchy which the world had ever known, was resolved to signalize his reign by extending still further the boundaries of his hereditary dominions. Asia was not enough to satisfy his boundless ambition. Europe must likewise be subjected to his power. His father's quarrel with the Greeks furnished him with a convenient apology for such enormous injustice. He spent four years in preparation for this great event, and Xerxes then ruled over the most fruitful portion of the globe, and the simple habits of life which then prevailed enabled the earth to sustain some three or four times the number that can be supported in the more costly and luxurious mode which has since been adopted by all civilized nations. He called upon every nation to furnish its quota of troops or ships or provisions, from Ethiopia to the Caspian, from the Aegean to the Persian Gulf. Four full years were consumed in making preparation, and all for what ? To crush a small nation.

"We naturally turn our eyes to Greece, the devoted object of all this expense. There she lies, with her beautiful islands laved by the crystal waters of the Aegean Sea. There is Athens, with her exquisite arts, her literature, and her science, with her constellations of genius just ready to burst upon the world. There was Sparta, less cultivated, but the bulwark of Grecian independence. There was Leonidas, with his three hundred. There, in a little peninsula, lay the intellectual hope of the world, the sole germ of free government forever and ever. Is this brave and gallant people to be crushed at a blow? Shall the Persian banners float on the hills of subjugate Greece ? Is it to be announced at Susa that order reigns in Attica? Is Asiatic despotism to overwhelm, in one long night of oppression, the very dawn of human greatness ? In that contest literature had her stake. The very existence of those men depended on the issue of this vast enterprise, whose works have been the study and delight of all succeeding time–that whole galaxy of genius, whose clustering radiance has since encircled the earth. The religion of our fathers had much at stake. Standing now and gazing back upon this epoch of history we are made to tremble, for all these were nations given to idolatry. Everywhere are ceremonies, temples, priests ; but both priest and people, the noble and the base, the learned and the simple, all alike grope in Cimmerian darkness as to the knowledge of the true God. There is but one exception to this in all the earth– the temple at Jerusalem. We turn our eyes eastward to Palestine, and there we see the temple of the true God just rising from the ruin of seventy years' desolation. Its builders, a feeble company, have just returned from a long captivity. The very language in which their holy oracles were written has become obsolete. Their speech is Chaldean, and their religious teachers are obliged from Sabbath to Sabbath to interpret from a dead language the records of their faith. This may answer for a small territory, and for a feeble few, as at that time, but the world needs light; and how shall the wisdom of God and the wisdom of man unite and carry God's wisdom round the world so that all may know the living and true God? If Xerxes prevail, this can never be. Forbid it, then, freedom ! Forbid it, then, religion ! Forbid it, intellect! Arise, O God, and let thine enemies be scattered, and those that rise up against the liberties of Thy people be driven away like the chaff which the wind driveth away. So Xerxes did not prevail ; the soil of Palestine would not bear the tread of a foe to the religion of the true God. The Jewish nature, breathing the invigorated air of freedom, disciplined by science, and animated and enlightened patriotism, grows up to a strength, a firmness and courage which hosts of slaves can never subdue, and by which the tenfold cord of oppression is rent asunder like the bands that bound the limbs of Samson. This army, though it was raised by Xerxes, is under the command of the God of heaven. It cannot, it must not, it shall not conquer. It is to teach the Greeks that they are masters of the world. It invites them to roll back the tide of conquest on Asia, and carry Grecian manners, arts, science, and language into the East. They shall penetrate to our holy land, into their language our holy oracles shall be translated; in their language shall be recorded the words of eternal life, and laden with the priceless treasure that language shall come back to Palestine, bearing light and truth and salvation to the nations and generations yet unborn. This diffusion of the Greek language took place by means of conquest. Although the action was man's, the ruling was God's; and that it entered into the divine plan of Providence we may know from the fact that it was a subject of prophecy. In a vision of Daniel, in Section 7, in the first year of Darius Hystaspes, it is written : 'Behold, there shall stand up three kings in Persia, and the fourth shall be far richer than them all ; and by his strength and through his riches he shall stir up all against the realm of Grecia.'

"Of this great attempt of Xerxes against Greece I have given account in my last letter. After the retreat of Xerxes into Asia, there was no attempt of the Greeks to make reprisals for many years. Unfortunately they were divided among themselves, and exhausted their energies in mutual quarrels. But the ages immediately succeeding the Persian invasion were the most wonderful in intellectual development that the world has ever seen. More great minds were produced within that century than in any other within the recorded history of our race. Providence seems to have kept back that wonderful nation until her intellectual treasure-house was full, and then to have sent her forth conquering and to conquer—not to destroy, but to fertilize the lands she overflowed ; not to extinguish civilization by barbarism, but to carry intellectual light to those who were sitting in the regions of ignorance and darkness. Nothing occurred of great interest between the Persians and the Greeks for nearly eighty years. The Greeks went on to create the most beautiful literature and the profoundest philosophy that human genius has ever produced, and their mutual contentions perfected them in the science and practice of war. At that time a circumstance took place which gave them a stronger proof of their great superiority over the Persians than even their victories over Xerxes. Cyrus the Younger was sent by his brother Artaxerxes to Asia Minor as the governor of the western provinces. Here he became acquainted with the martial valor of the Greeks, and thought by their aid to march to Susa and dethrone his brother. For this purpose he collected an army of more than one hundred thousand, thirteen thousand of whom were Greeks, and advanced into the plains of the East. He was there met by his brother with an army of nine hundred thousand, defeated, and left dead on the field. The thirteen thousand Greeks, now reduced to ten thousand, found themselves two thousand miles from the nearest Grecian city where they would be safe, without one day's provisions, in the midst of an enemy's country. Undismayed by this most appalling condition, they commenced their retreat, cut their way through enemies in front, and guarded themselves from foes in the rear. They went over mountains covered with snow, through trackless forests, and over rivers rapid and deep, and reached their homes in safety. This exploit filled the world with their fame, and perhaps more than anything else convinced the Greeks that, few as they were, they held the destinies of Asia at their disposal. But confederated republics, however efficient for defence, are generally ill-calculated for conquest. It was not till more than forty years after this, when all Greece had been subjected to Philip, King of Macedonia, that the nation turned its eyes to the conquest of the East. Philip had himself elected general-in-chief of all the Greeks for the prosecution of the war with their ancient enemies, the Persians. Just at the moment when the conqueror of

Greece was meditating a descent upon the Persian Empire, he fell by the hand of an assassin, leaving his kingdom to his son Alexander, a youth of twenty. This happened three hundred and eighty years ago, and may be considered as one of the great epochs of the world."

Fourth Letter.

"Alexander, by his personal endowments as conqueror and statesman, did more in twelve years to affect the future condition of the world than any uninspired man that has ever lived. He was in no respect better than his modern rivals, and was animated by no better motive than personal ambition. In the hands of God he was used as an instrument of lasting good to mankind. Endowed with an intellect of unusual power and comprehension, he received a thorough education from one of the greatest philosophers that ever lived. At the age of eighteen he, began to mingle affairs of state with study, and became a soldier as well as a scholar. At the age of twenty, when summoned to assume the reins of empire–the sovereign, in fact, of the Greeks–he stood before the world a perfect representative of his nation. He combined their genius and learning with their valor and conduct; and entering Asia with the sword in one hand and the poems of Homer in the other, he became the armed leader of Grecian learning, art, and civilization. Wherever he went Greece went with him. His conquests were not so much those of Macedonian arms as of Grecian letters. Wherever he went, he took with him the genius of Homer, the sublime soul of Plato, and the practical wisdom of Socrates; and not only monarchies sprung up in his wake, but schools of philosophy and academies of learning.

Entering Asia with an army of thirty-five thousand men, in the space of twelve years he made himself master of the whole Persian Empire, and of many nations which had never been subjected to the Persian yoke. He carried the Grecian language and manners to the Indus, and subjected to his power nearly as large a portion of the human race as there was in existence. His first battle gave him Asia Minor.

The second all of Syria to the Euphrates; Egypt, the whole valley of the Nile, surrendered without striking a blow. The third great battle, on the banks of the Euphrates, opened to him the whole of the Asiatic plains to the mountains which bounded the habitations of the Scythian tribes. Wherever he went the Greek language and literature took up their abode, and every city on this side the Euphrates in a few ages became the residence of Greek philosophers, poets, rhetoricians, grammarians, historians, till the whole circuitous shore of the Mediterranean became almost as Grecian as Greece herself. Our beloved Palestine, of course, came under his sway, and the influence of his career on the fortunes of us Jews was more decisive, perhaps, than upon any other nation, for it was his conquest alone which introduced the Greek language into our holy land. And so much do the most important events turn on the slightest causes, that on the chances of one life, almost daily exposed to destruction by the dangers of war, depended the issue whether the records of the holy oracles should ever be sent to the perishing world through this beautiful language. It has been declared that when the mighty warrior and statesman was approaching Jerusalem, Judua, who was our high priest at that time, came out to meet him in solemn procession, and that Alexander was so struck by his appearance, that he not only spared the city, but granted to us Jews many favors that he did not show to others, giving as a reason therefor that he had seen the same person in a dream before He left Macedonia, who had assured him of the conquest of the Persian empire.

"From Syria he passed on to Egypt, and his conquest of that country had a greater influence upon the future condition of our nation than the conquest of Judea itself: for on his return from Ethiopia he sailed down the western branch of the Nile, and, with the instinct of genius, fixed upon the site of a city between the lake Mareotis and the sea, which he called after his own name. It sprung up immediately to be one of the most magnificent cities of the world, reigning as a sort of queen of the East, as the mart of commerce and the seat of wealth. To people this city we Jews were invited by the most liberal offers. A large colony was formed, where only the Greek language was used. Hence, it became necessary to have our Scriptures translated into Greek, or we would have lost our knowledge of them altogether. It is said on good authority that the occasion of translating the Scriptures into the Greek language was the desire of Ptolemy Philadelphus to have a copy to go into the Alexandrian library, which was begun not long after his death. However that might be, such a version we know was made, which is now the standard of the world. It was made about three hundred years ago, and by this translation our theology has gone to the whole world. Thus we see that Divine Providence works the nations of the earth like a machine.

"Another important factor in God's providence is the rising of the Roman Empire. While all these things were transpiring in the East, a nation was rising into notice in the south of Italy destined to exert a more extensive influence upon the world by her arms than Greece did by her learning. About seven hundred and fifty years ago a small band of refugees from the ruins of Troy joined other adventurers, and established themselves on the banks of the Tiber. Their government at first was monarchical. They were poor in resources, temperate and frugal in their habits, but, either from choice or necessity, warlike from the first. Italy was not then a new nor an uncultivated country. It must have contained states and cities of great wealth, for there have been discovered vast receptacles for the dead dating back much earlier than the time of Romulus. These were a nation of soldiers and statesmen, trained from their earliest years to politics and war. Their monarchy lasted about two hundred years. While that lasted there was little indication that these Romans were to become the masters of the world. The establishment of a popular government, however, rapidly developed their national characteristics—a love of conquest and military glory. This character once formed, and all honor and promotion coming from the people, none could hope to succeed without bending the whole force of his talents to that object which every citizen had most at heart—the honor of the Roman name, and the extension of their dominions over foreign nations. The Senate, composed either of the most distinguished and influential of the citizens, or of those who had made their way through the regular grades of the magistracy to the highest which was known in the State, constituted a body, which, for more than a thousand years, for talent, for weight, for wisdom and experience, was unrivalled in the history of the world. The Roman from youth to age lived in the eye of his country. To gain the favor of the arbiters of his destiny was his perpetual study and his constant endeavor. Thus from the first, every faculty was put upon the utmost stretch, and nothing was omitted through the whole course of his education which could give him eloquence before the people, valor and conduct in the field, and wisdom in the Senate. The whole nation was a sort of military school. No man could be a candidate for office until he had served his country ten years as a soldier in the camp. The result was that, by thus bending all the powers of human nature in one direction, they excelled all mankind in that art to which they were exclusively devoted. They became a nation of soldiers, and, pursuing with steady aim and untiring perseverance one exclusive object for eight centuries, they naturally became the conquerors of the world. A Roman army was the most terrible object that ever trod the earth, it was a vast human machine contrived for the subjugation of the world, instinct with intelligence, shielded from assault by an almost impenetrable armor, and animated with a courage which was best displayed in the shock of battle. When we hear of a Roman camp, we cease to wonder how that nation carried conquest from the sands of Africa to the borders of the world, to the skirts of the Arabian desert. After the age of seventeen, every Roman was liable to be enrolled and sent to the war at any time.

When he arrived at the camp he entered on a course of life in which ease and luxury were altogether unknown. He commenced a discipline of hardships that is almost incredible, and of which there was no end; and with all this training it took the Romans five hundred years to conquer Italy; it took two hundred more and they were masters of the known world.

"About one hundred years ago the Roman conquest reached our holy land. Pompey the Great polluted with impious tread the holy of holies, and the Roman legions planted their standard upon the rampart of the temple. About seventy years ago Caesar subjected the liberties of his country, putting an end to the republic which had existed four hundred years; and fifty years ago all the world was given peace. Thus it is that the Grecian letters and Roman arms were founded on the mission of Moses; also the Roman statesman was made quite as subservient to the great plan of Providence as the valor of the Roman commanders ; for they alone of all nations that ever existed were able to retain and consolidate their conquests. Their polity, perfected by the experience of ages, greatly alleviated the burden of their yoke, and it is often said that after conquering like savages they ruled like sages; and if it is objected: how can God's providence permit so many minds to come under a rule so hostile to liberty and freedom ? To this I reply: the governments destroyed are always worse than the ones set up in their place, though it may not always be seen by man."

Fifth Letter.

"Man is essentially a human being. He is made so

by the faculties of his mind, as well as the emotions of his heart. He is so both by the intellectual and moral nature. One of the first and most spontaneous exercises of the reason of man is the investigation of cause and effect, and one of the first convictions which are developed in the mind is that there cannot be an effect without a cause. The next is, that the nature of a cause must correspond with the nature of the effect, and can certainly be known by it. It is so in the works of man. When we see an exquisite painting it is impossible for us to doubt its having been the creation of intelligence. When Aristippus was cast on a shore where there appeared to be no inhabitants, he wandered about until he found some mathematical diagrams traced in the sand.

'Courage," said he, 'my friend ; I find the traces of men.' And so I say to the wandering and forsaken Jews of God : Courage ; I see the finger of God pointing. Men see in everything the traces of power and wisdom. Nay, we know that we are the effects of superior power and wisdom. Unbelief has not prevailed much in the world, and it has been quite as rare among the heathen as among those who have had a revelation. So much for abstract religious convictions.

"Men are led to God by their understanding and by their moral nature. On the first dawn of his faculties man experiences within him certain moral perceptions. This is right, meritorious, honorable ; that is wrong, base, despicable, worthy of punishment. This moral nature he finds exists not only in himself, but in others. It is a universal attribute of man. It is not a fortuitous endowment. It is given to man by his Creator as the law of his action. It can come from no other source. But the moral power in man is only the faculty to see them because they exist. Then God sees them and they are realities, and He created both them and us. Our consciousness of the power to choose between the good and the bad creates within us a sense of responsibility to the being that made us.

Connected with this idea of God, which seems to be necessary and universal, is that of a providence, an intelligence which not only made the world but governs it ; which, therefore, knows the past, the present, and the future, and which, of course, observes not only all that is seen by mortal eyes, but likewise all that passes in the human mind. Men have seen that the general course of events is, that vice should be punished and virtue rewarded ; vice, therefore, is regarded by God with displeasure; and as He now punishes it, so He will continue to do. As a good man now and ever must be the object of His approbation, and as God is infinite in power, the good man will be forever rewarded. Such are the natural convictions of mankind, which result from the operations of his own mind. Such are the convictions of the heathen world. The great men of the old world, poets and philosophers, have entertained such opinions in all time. They all take for granted one superior being and all others inferior beings that are responsible to Him. This is not only the last and highest conclusion of human intellect, but likewise the consenting voice of the most ancient tradition.

"But then, even in the best minds the subject was surrounded with great doubt and difficulties. God Himself is an object of none of the senses. It is in vain, therefore, for the human mind to form an idea of the mode of His existence. Not being, then, a matter of sense or of demonstration, the wisest of men, though he might arrive at the truth, could not feel sure that it was truth. Wanting certainty himself, he could not impart certainty to others. He could not propagate his doctrine with confidence. The wisest of men, therefore, wanted that authority which was requisite even for the propagation of the truth. They wanted certainty for themselves and authority for others. Now, certainty and authority are the very things which are necessary to make a religion powerful in the world. While religion, therefore, was in the hands of the philosophers (that is, the thinkers), it effected next to nothing in guiding and restraining mankind, it being merely a matter of opinion–that is, of dim probability. One man felt that he had just as good a right to his opinion as another. One philosopher differed from another, and thus weakened the authority of the opinions of both. A religion, therefore, in the true sense of the word–that is, one that shall take hold of the future and control the conduct of mankind–must have certainly and authority. Neither of these can be obtained without revelation, inspiration, and miracles.

"Had Moses himself received no divine aid, either from inspiration or miracles, even if he had uttered the same truths and laid down the same precepts, he would have accomplished nothing in the world. His doctrines would have rested for evidence on his own reason, and his precepts upon his own personal character and influence. Another man of equal wisdom and the same weight of character might have overthrown what he had built up. Besides, his manner would have been entirely different. No man can inspire confidence in others who has not confidence in himself. No man in high religious matters can have full confidence in himself without conscious divine inspiration. It was reasonable, therefore, in him, when sent by God into Egypt to bring out his enslaved brethren, to demand miraculous credentials and without them he could neither have brought them out nor established among them the religion he was commissioned to teach. This distinction was perceived by the people, though the reason upon which it was founded was beyond their comprehension. The difference arose from the difference between knowledge and opinion. One is necessarily proposed with diffidence ; the other with confidence, which no one uninspired can counterfeit. Those who knew best about these things among the heathen had no means of guiding the multitude. But then mankind must have a religion. The understanding demands it, and the heart craves it. It is not with the multitude as with the philosophers, a matter of quiet contemplation. They must act as well as think and feel. The sentiments of the heart demand expression, and expression they will have, through the actions of the hands, and through the words of the mouth. Occasions were continually occurring demanding immediate action. Some public calamity bowed down the hearts of thousands, and seemed to indicate the wrath of superior powers. Those powers must be supplicated and appealed. Who shall contrive the rite ? Not the wisest, but the man of the greatest boldness and readiness of invention. Once established, proscription took the place of reason, and habit consecrated that which was at first wanting in propriety.

"Then, again, religion has much to do with imagination. Everything relating to God is invisible. There is nothing positively to determine and fix our ideas; but in pure spirituality our imagination finds no play, nothing to lay hold of. Still it is impossible to keep them quiet, even in our most solemn devotions, and perhaps it has been found absolutely impossible for the most spiritual man altogether to separate the idea of corporiety from God.

"How much more impossible, then, must it have been for the uninstructed heathen, with the best intentions ? Therefore, there must have been diversities and great imperfection in heathen opinions and heathen worship. Such we find to have been the fact. Certain of the existence of a God, yet uncertain of the mode of His existence, it was natural that the human mind should run into a thousand vagaries and a thousand errors. It was natural that mankind should fancy that they had found God in those parts of the material universe where His attributes are most displayed. Hence, the most ancient species of idolatry is said to have been that which deified the heavenly bodies, the sun and moon and the hosts of heaven. The sun is perhaps the brightest emblem of God, except the human soul. To us he is, in fact, the mightiest instrument, as it were, the right hand of the benignity of the Most High. He riseth, and the shadows of night flee away. Joy and beauty go forth to meet him in the morning. At his call universal life riseth, as it were, from a universal death. He draweth aside the curtains of darkness and sayeth unto man, Come forth ! He shineth, and the face of nature is glad. He hideth his face, and all things mourn. He withdraweth from the western sky, and darkness resumes her ancient dominion, and all things seem to wait his return. The soul itself, as it were, deprived of its support, gradually loses its energies, and sinks into a profound repose. What wonder, then, that in the native ignorance of mankind of the true nature of God, the wise should have worshipped the sun as the fittest emblem of God, and the ignorant as God Himself. Such was probably the idolatry of the nations from among whom Abraham was called to the worship of the true God. Such was the worship of the Chaldeans and Egyptians. It is a record of the Talmud that Abraham, when returning from the grotto where he was born to the city of Babylon, gazed on a certain star, 'Behold,' said he, 'the God, the Lord of the universe.' But as he gazed the star sank away and was gone, and Abraham felt that the Lord was unchangeable, and he was deceived. Again, the full moon appeared, and he said, 'This is our God ;' but the moon withdrew and he was deceived. All the rest of the night he spent in profound meditation. At sun rise he stood before the gates of Babylon, and saw all the people prostrate before the rising sun. 'Wondrous orb,' he exclaimed, ' thou surely art the creator and ruler of nations, but thou, like the rest, hasteneth away, so the Creator is somewhere else.' How much more sublime, as well as rational, the doctrine which he originated, and the sentiments which were afterward expressed by one of his followers, which make these glorious orbs only the manifestations of something far more glorious than they!

"One great source of corruption was the priesthood. It seems natural that men should be chosen to conduct religious service. They became better acquainted with these rites than others, and are more sacred by the power of association which renders their ministration more satisfactory, and, of course, more profitable to those in whose behalf they perform sacred offices. A priesthood seemed to be so necessary, but there is nothing more dangerous to a nation than to have a priesthood that is governed by the political parties of the nation, as was done by all nations except our own. Here the priest was governed by the laws of Moses, and it was impossible for the priest or anybody else to change them. It is to be attributed to these heathen priests that idolatry is so common. Go down into Egypt, and you find men worshipping an ox. Cats and crocodiles occupy the places of the inferior gods, and are worshipped by the poor. Thus in all nations, except our own, this dreadful state of idolatry prevails. The idolatry of Greece is no better. Athens contains many statues erected to imaginary gods. Her superstition is not only bigoted but bloody. It was there that Socrates suffered death merely on suspicion of maintaining opinions subversive of the popular faith."

Sixth Letter.

"The end of all religion as a positive institution is to enlighten the understanding and cultivate the devotions. The mind must think and the heart must worship. So it must be through life. The cares of the world are continually effacing religious impressions, and truths once clearly seen and vividly felt by lapse of time wax dim and lose the influence of present realities. The soul, moreover, feels the want of support and guidance of religion at all times. Every day the soul experiences the need of communion with God. It is as necessary as our daily food. Therefore, all religion has its sacred rites, by which the heart speaks to God and God communicates to the heart. So all religions have some mode of training the mind and moving the affections, of taking hold of the memory and perpetuating themselves. This is derived from an innate consciousness. If God should extinguish all the lights of the world and blind every human eye, religion would be just the same.

"But these outward institutions must all be adapted to the present condition of man. Religion can only use those instruments which are furnished to hand. In the absence of writing it must use ceremonies and forms, which have a conventional meaning, and thus come to be symbolic of certain truths. Thus, our patriarchal religion consisted almost entirely of prayer and sacrifice, The Mosaic religion, which came after the invention of letters, added to prayer and sacrifice a written code of duty, a formal declaration of truths and principles, which lay at the foundation of the whole institution.

"The patriarchal element was still strong and predominant in all our Church, yet there was no express mode of religious instruction. This was enjoined on the heads of families: 'And these words which I command thee this day, thou shalt teach them to thy children, and shalt talk of them when thou sittest in thy house.' And as the written laws were scarce and hard to get, it was said: 'And thou shalt bind them for a sign upon thine hand and as frontlets between thine eyes, and thou shalt write them upon the posts of thine house and upon thy gates.'

Then the Levites were to stand and say with a loud voice: 'Cursed be the man that maketh any graven image and all the people shall hold up their hands and say, amen; and thus he went through the whole law. Then at the annual meeting upon the mountains at new moon all the people met and held up their hands and cried, amen. Thus it is evident that devotion predominated over instruction ; the cultivation of the heart was made more prominent than that of the understanding.

"But in the Hebrew commonwealth Church and State were closely amalgamated. The code of Moses prescribed a like religious and civil duty. The Levites, of course, were the judges and magistrates, as well as the religious teachers of the people. But as books were scarce, we find in the third year of the reign of Jehoshaphat that he sent princes and Levites to teach the people, and they took the book of the law and went through all the cities of Judea and taught the people the law of the Lord.

"This same thing was carried out in all the Jewish life. Our tabernacle in the wilderness, and afterward in the holy land, was intended as a perpetual memorial of God, and a symbol of His presence. It called the people off from idolatry, and reminded them that their worship was to be directed to Jehovah alone. Its services, and those afterward of the temple, were perpetually renewed every morning and every evening, that no pious Israelite should ever feel that the duties of adoration and gratitude could be omitted for a single day. The morning and evening sacrifice, we have every reason to believe, was to the religiously disposed an essential aid to devotion through the many centuries of the continuance of that imposing rite.

"Then if we transfer these imposing ceremonies to the temple, this godly house was the rallying point of our political power, the consecrated seat of our religion, and the heart of our national affections. It was built by Solomon more than a thousand years ago. It was built on Mount Moriah, in the southeastern part of Jerusalem. It was built for worship alone. It was intended as a place for national worship. It consisted of four enclosures, one within another on three sides, but having a common wall on the fourth, Only one of these was covered with a roof, in our meaning of the term, and that was the last or innermost enclosure–the holy of holies, containing the ark, the cherubim, and the mercy seat. The outer enclosure, into which all nations were permitted to enter, was very large. The second was the court of women–so-called, not because none but women were permitted to enter there, but because they were permitted to go no further. Within this was the court of Israel, which again surrounded on three sides that of the priests, where was the great altar, upon which the daily sacrifice was offered morning and evening.

"Oh, these sacred ordinances! How can the world do without them ? It seems that the world could do as well without the light of the sun, as well without food to eat or water to drink, as to do without these doctrines and teachings of the Jews. But they are all gone. The city, the temple, the doctrine, the priest, the law, and the nation are all gone. Is it so that God has become tired of His own appointments? or does He see a defect in His own ways, or has He become dissatisfied with His own covenant made to our fathers and to their children ?

"I write you these letters, my beloved countrymen,

asking you to look at these things, and find out the cause of our abandonment. Is it the cause that sent our fathers into Egypt ? or is it caused by the same thing that sent them into Babylon ? Let us look and find out the cause, so that we may seek a remedy. And let us not forget the morning and evening sacrifice. Let us turn our faces toward that holy temple and pray. Although it is not in existence in fact, yet it lives in each of our hearts, and shall ever live. Though we may be thousands of miles away, and be sold into bondage, and bound in chains, yet we will not, we cannot, forget our land, our religion, and our God. He is the God of Abraham, and still is merciful, and will remember His promises and keep His covenant made with our fathers. And so shall I abide."

Seventh Letter.

THE EXPECTATION OF THE JEWS.

Not only was the expectation of a remarkable personage universally prevalent among the Jews at the time of the appearance of Christ, but the phraseology was already in use which designated what he was to be and accomplish. There was at the time of Christ a Messianic phraseology derived from different parts of the Old Testament, which embodied and expressed all their anticipations. Whatever inspiration accompanied the first composition of the prophecies, there was evidently none in their interpretation. This much was certain, that there was to be a Messiah, there was to be a new dispensation. No one knew precisely what he was to be. Imagination, of course, was set to work, and each one for himself formed his own, and made whatever passage of the Old Testament he choose to be descriptive of his person and office. Not only the imagination, but the passions were concerned in the formation of their expectations. The pious thought of him as a religious reformer, and the new state of things to be a condition of higher religious perfection. The rabbis interpreted concerning the days of the Messiah such passages as this from the 31st chapter of Jeremiah, "Behold, the days come, saith the Lord, that I will make a new covenant with the house of Israel and with the house of Judah. Not according to the covenant that I made with their fathers in the day that I took them by the hand to bring them out of the land of Egypt. But this shall be the covenant that I will make with the house of Israel. After those days, saith the Lord, I will put my law in their inward parts, and write it on their hearts, and will be their God, and they shall be my people. And they shall teach no more every man his neighbors and every man his brother, saying, Know the Lord, for they all shall know me, from the least of them even unto the greatest of them, saith the Lord ; for I will forgive their iniquity and remember their sin no more.' This seems to have been the expectation entertained by the Samaritans, if the woman with whom Christ talked at the well of Jacob is to be considered as speaking the sentiments of the nation.

"The universal expectation seems to have been that he was to be a prophet like unto Moses, but greater. In accordance with this sentiment Peter, in one of his first discourses after the resurrection of Jesus, cites the promise of Moses to the Israelites just before his death, as applicable to Christ. 'A prophet shall the Lord your

God raise up unto you of your brethren like unto me, him shall ye hear in all things whatsoever he shall say unto you. And it shall come to pass that every soul which shall not hear the prophet shall be destroyed from among the people.' These were the sentiments of those who had seen the miracle of feeding the five thousand with a few loaves and fishes, bearing so strong a resemblance to the feeding of the Israelites in the desert. Then those men when they had seen the miracle which Jesus did, said: 'This is of a truth that prophet that should come into the world.'

Another and much larger class gave the Messianic prophecies a more worldly meaning. The great personage whose coming they shortly expected was to be a king, but greater than any who had sat upon the Jewish throne. It was with this expectation evidently that his disciples followed him through his whole ministry. And even after his resurrection they seem for awhile to have entertained the same hopes. One of the first questions which they asked him after he rose was: 'Wilt thou at this time restore the kingdom to Israel?' And at the last supper they disputed 'which of them should be the greatest,' that is, who should be highest in office in the new kingdom that he was about to set up. It was with this idea that he was hailed by the multitude into Jerusalem with the shout, 'Hosanna to the son of David.' This was the idea which Nathaniel meant to express when he said, on receiving the evidence that he was a prophet: 'Rabbi, thou art the Son of God, thou art the king of Israel.' That it was his temporal character to which Nathaniel here referred we have sufficient evidence in the information which first directed his attention to Jesus. 'We have found him of whom Moses in the law and the prophets did write, Jesus of Nazareth, the son of Joseph.' The part of the Old Testament from which this title and expectation were taken was principally the second Psalm. The person described in this poem is represented as exalted by God to be a king on Mount Zion in Judea. The surrounding heathen are represented as being enraged. But God has nevertheless determined that he shall reign ; and as a king sets his son upon his throne while he yet lives, so has God, as Supreme King of Israel, exalted this person to share His authority, and pledges His own power to support his throne.

"One idea of the kingdom of the Messiah, derived from this Psalm, was that he was not only to reign over the Jews, but destroy all other nations. 'Why do the heathen rage and the people imagine a vain thing. The kings of the earth set themselves, and the rulers take counsel together against the Lord, and against his Anointed, saying, Let us break their bands asunder, and cast away their cords from us. He that sitteth in the heavens shall laugh. The Lord shall have them in derision. Then shall He speak to them in his wrath, and vex them in his sore displeasure. Yet I have set my king upon my holy hill of Zion. I will declare the decree, the Lord hath said unto me. Thou art my son, this day have I begotten thee. Ask of me, and I will give thee the heathen for thine inheritance, and the uttermost parts of the earth for a possession. Thou shalt break them with a rod of iron, thou shalt dash them in pieces like a potter's vessel.' This Psalm was interpreted by the Jews almost universally of the Messiah, and the more readily as the title Anointed is translated in the Septuagint *Christos* so that it there reads, 'Against the Lord and against His Christ.' The Messiah, therefore, was to reign on Mount Zion, one of the mountains on which Jerusalem was built, and reign over the Jews and by God's assistance subdue the heathen by war and conquest, break them with a rod of iron, and dash them in pieces as a potter's vessel. Such was the kingdom which the great majority of the Jews expected their Messiah to set up.

"The phrase, ' kingdom of heaven,' is taken from the second chapter of the Book of Daniel. After foretelling that there should arise four great monarchies, the Babylonian, the Persian, the Grecian, and the Roman, the last of which should be a kingdom of iron, he goes on to say, 'And in the days of these kings shall the God of heaven set up a kingdom which shall never be destroyed, and the kingdom shall not be left to other people, but it shall break in pieces, and consume all these kingdoms, and it shall stand forever.' In another passage : 'I saw in the night a vision, and behold, one like the Son of Man came with the clouds of heaven, and came to the Ancient of days, and they brought him near before him. And there was given unto him dominion, and glory, and a kingdom, that all people, nations, and languages should serve him. His dominion is an everlasting dominion, and his kingdom that which shall not be destroyed.'

"From this last passage was probably derived the opinion once held, that the Messiah should never die. Jesus said on a certain occasion : 'And I, if I be lifted up from the earth, will draw all men unto me.' The people answered him, 'We have heard out of the law that Christ abideth forever ; and how sayest thou the Son of Man must be lifted up? Who is this Son of Man ?' The new dispensation under the figure of a kingdom was the subject of the commencing petition of one of the chief prayers recited in their synagogues, from Sabbath to Sabbath, and has been so for ages. There was a time specified in the Book of Daniel of seventy weeks, which was to intervene between the building of the second temple and the times of the Messiah, which, interpreting according to the prophetic style, a day for a year, would bring the period of his appearance somewhere near the time when John the Baptist began to preach.

"So prevalent had this expectation become that it had spread beyond the holy land. Tacitus, a historian who wrote in Italy, records the fact that among many 'there was a persuasion that in the ancient books of the priesthood it was written that at this precise time the East should become mighty, and that those issuing from Judea should rule the world.' Suetonius, another Latin historian, writes 'that in the East an ancient and constant opinion prevailed that it was fated there should issue at this time from Judea those who should obtain universal dominion.'

"This confident expectation of the Jews had already caused no little political disturbance. It was this proud anticipation of universal conquest which made them so restive under the government of the Romans. That they who were destined to reign over the world–and whose King Messiah was to have the heathen for his inheritance, the uttermost parts of the earth for his possession, who was to break with a rod of iron, and dash them in pieces like a potter's vessel–should be in vassalage to a foreign power, was more than they could bear. Josephus relates that about the time of the birth of Christ, when Cyrenius was sent to take a census of Judea, Judas, a native of Gamala in Galilee, rose up and resisted the Roman commissioner, and raised a great rebellion. He is mentioned likewise by Gamaliel in his speech before the Jewish Sanhedrim, when the apostles were brought before them for preaching Jesus as the Messiah, immediately after his ascension. 'After this man, rose up Judas of Galilee, in the days of taxing, and drew away much people after him ; he also perished, and all, as many as obeyed him, were dispersed.' Josephus speaks generally of the troubles of those times, without specifying their causes. And now Judea was full of robberies, and as the several companies of the seditious would light upon anyone to head them he was created a king immediately, in order to do mischief to the public.

"This was exactly the state of the country during the ministry of Jesus, and it explains his caution in proclaiming himself the Messiah, and his withdrawal as soon as a multitude collected about him and manifested any tendency to sedition or disturbance. It is recorded of him, that, after the miracle of feeding the five thousand, and the declaration made concerning him, 'This of a truth is that prophet which should come into the world.' When Jesus therefore perceived that they would come and take him by force, and make him a king, he departed again into a mountain himself alone.' In another instance, likewise, when he had healed the man at the pool of Bethesda, 'And he that was healed wist not who it was; for Jesus had conveyed himself away, a multitude being in that place.'

"Such being the expectation of the Jews, as we learn

from profane history, a man of singular habits and appearance began to preach in a retired part of Judea, where there were but few large towns: ' Repent, for the kingdom of heaven is at hand.' This man was of the sacerdotal tribe, and had been consecrated to God from his infancy by the vow of the Nazarite. His habits and dress were those of a hermit, his food such as he could pick up in the fields and woods. He was literally the voice of one crying in the wilderness, 'Prepare ye the way of the Lord. Make straight in the desert a highway for our God.' He professed to have been moved by divine impulse to proclaim the immediate approach of the Messiah. A man of such singular appearance, bearing such an important message, produced a great sensation, and excited the strongest curiosity. Crowds from all parts of Judea flocked together to see and hear him. Some thought that he was the Messiah. His fame soon reached Jerusalem, and the Jewish authorities sent a deputation of priests and Levites to inquire who he was. He told them that he was not the Messiah, but was sent to introduce him. 'I came to point him out to Israel.' Here was undoubtedly stated the true reason why he was raised up by Divine Providence to prepare the Jewish mind for the great message from God which they were about to receive, to shape their ideas from the crude mass of traditions which had existed among them into some resemblance to the dispensation that the Messiah was about to establish. 'There was a man sent from God whose name was John. The same came for a witness, that all men through him might believe. He was not the Light, but was sent to bear witness of the Light.'

"The effect of his preaching was precisely what was

intended. He produced a strong impression upon the public mind, and, though he wrought no miracle, all men held him to be a prophet. He presented a strong contrast, and probably by design, to the pretenders to divine mission who appeared about that time. It was on this account that the multitudes which gathered about him created no uneasiness in the public authorities. A man, like John, who clothed himself in the coarsest attire, in a country where the higher classes were studious of ornament, and all who had any pretensions to official dignity were distinguished by gorgeous apparel, would naturally escape all suspicion of political ambition. A religious teacher evidently sincere and pious, and withal free from fanaticism and enthusiasm, after the cessation of prophecy for four hundred years, must have produced a great impression. He must have recalled to the minds of his countrymen the days when Elijah in a like simplicity and grave austerity stood up as a prophet of God, and the champion of religion. Some, indeed, mistook him for Elijah risen from the dead, who, their traditions affirmed, was to come to anoint and inaugurate the Messiah. The almost simultaneous appearance of the Light, and the witness to the Light, without any concert or collusion, was a strong testimony to the divine mission of both. With this argument alone Jesus on one occasion silenced those who questioned his claim to be the Messiah. 'The baptism of John, whence was it ? From heaven or of men?' They reasoned among themselves, saying: 'If we say of heaven, then he will say, Why then did ye not believe on him ?' and, of course, believe on him to whom he bore witness. 'But if we say of men, the people will stone us, for all counted John as a prophet.' It does not appear that John had any particular person in his mind when he commenced his mission, but was merely informed by God, who sent him to preach, that the Messiah should be pointed out to him by some miraculous appearance. He had known him before as a person of great piety and excellence : for when Jesus came to him to be baptized, John said to him, 'I have need to be baptized of thee, and comest thou to me ?' But as the Messiah he had no knowledge of him, for he testifies, "I knew him not,' that is, as the Messiah, 'but He that sent me to baptize with water, the same said unto me: Upon whom thou shalt see the Spirit descending and remaining on him, the same is he that shall baptize with the Holy Ghost.' John collected around him a company of disciples whom he instructed in the mysteries of religion, and many of them seem to have remained with him after he was cast into prison, till he was beheaded by Herod.

"We have reason to conclude, I think, that his teaching shadowed forth, though imperfectly, the general system of Christianity. Jesus says of him, 'That among them that are born of women, there hath not arisen a greater prophet than John the Baptist,' and they bear a strong resemblance to the opening discourses of Christ. 'And the people said unto him, What shall we do then ? He answered and said unto them, He that hath two coats, let him impart unto him that hath none, and he that hath meat, let him do likewise.' 'Then came the taxgatherers to be baptized, and said unto him, Master, what shall we do? And he said unto them, Exact no more than is appointed you. And the soldiers likewise demanded of him, saying, And what shall we do? And he said unto them, Do violence to no man, neither accuse any falsely, and be content with your wages.'

"That John preached the essential doctrines of Christianity would appear from what we read, 'And a certain Jew, named Apollos, born in Alexandria, an eloquent man and mighty in the Scriptures, came to Ephesus. This man was instructed in the way of the Lord, and, being fervent in spirit, he spake and taught diligently the things of the Lord, knowing only the baptism of John. And he began to speak boldly in the synagogue, whom when Aquilla and Priscilla had heard they took him unto them, and expounded to him the way of the Lord more perfectly.' In the nineteenth chapter: 'And it came to pass that while Apollos was at Corinth, Paul, having passed through the upper coasts, came to Ephesus, and finding certain disciples, he said unto them, Have ye received the Holy Ghost since ye believed? And they said unto him, We have not so much as heard whether there be any Holy Ghost. And he said unto them, Unto what then were ye baptized? And they said, Unto John's baptism.' Now, here are two cases in which those who had heard nothing but the doctrines of John are said to have been Christians, to have been taught the things of the Lord, and to have been disciples.

"It follows then, of course, that John the Baptist taught the essential truths of Christianity. The object of the gospels being to record the teaching of Jesus, that of John is passed over in a very cursory manner. But that he taught often and much, as well as prophesied the coming of the Messiah, we have every reason to believe. His disciples, however, mingled some of the old forms with their new doctrines, for they fasted often, an observance which Jesus declared agreed no better with the new religion than a piece of new cloth with an old garment, or new wine with old bottles.

"The mind of John the Baptist furnishes a remarkable example, which we often meet with, of partial divine illumination, the clearest knowledge on some points, and absolute ignorance on others. By the light of inspiration be shadowed forth in a few words the nature of the kingdom of heaven, whose approach he foretold, and showed it to be something entirely different from the expectation of the Jews, handed down from remote ages; yet of its details his ideas seem to have been vague, and he appears to have had no certain knowledge that Jesus was the Messiah, though he had baptized him and received the heavenly sign of which they had been forewarned.

"One truth which he announced bears evident marks of supernatural origin–since it contradicted the conceptions and prejudices of the age–that the Messiah and his kingdom were not to be national, not belonging of right and exclusion to the posterity of Abraham alone. There is a maxim, as common as the very letters of the alphabet, in the writings of the rabbis, that 'There is a part for all Israel in the world to come,' that is, in the kingdom of Messiah, merely by virtue of their descent from Abraham. That it was to be a kingdom selected from Israel and other nations, a new community by no means coextensive with the seed of Abraham, they had not the slightest idea. That it was to be a moral and a spiritual kingdom was as far from their conceptions. 'Repent, for the kingdom of God is at hand. Bring forth, therefore, fruits worthy of repentance. And say not, we have Abraham for our father, for God is able of these stones to raise up children to Abraham.' Think not that you are to belong to the kingdom of God merely because you are descended from Abraham. God is able to raise up children to Abraham from a source now as improbable to you as the stones beneath your feet, from among the Gentiles even, whom you are accustomed to call dogs, and count as the offscouring of the earth. A discrimination is about to take place, not between the children of Abraham and other nations, but between the good and the bad even among the Jews themselves. 'The axe lieth at the root of all the trees. Every tree therefore, which bringeth not forth good fruit is hewn down and cast into the fire. I indeed baptize you with water, but he that cometh after me is mightier than I, whose shoes I am not worthy to bear, he shall baptize you with the Holy Ghost and with fire.' He shall raise those who obey him to a higher degree of spiritual knowledge, perfection, and power, and punish those who disobey him with the severest suffering. 'Whose winnowing fan is in his hand, and he will thoroughly purge his grain, and gather the wheat into his garner, but he will burn up the chaff with unquenchable fire.' This is the same idea expressed in stronger language, the meaning of which is this, The Messiah's kingdom is not, as you Jews expect, to comprehend the good and the bad merely because they are the descendants of Abraham, but is to embrace the good only, who are to be gathered into a separate community, while the bad are to be abandoned to the destruction which their own wicked courses will inevitably bring upon them.

"He not only preached the kingdom of God as a

separate society, distinct from the Jewish nation, but he actually began to set it up. The baptism which he instituted was no idle, unmeaning form, nor did it signify simply a profession of repentance, but it began and founded a new community. Those who received it professed not only repentance as necessary to prepare them for the kingdom of the Messiah, now shortly expected to appear, but a readiness to believe in and obey him whenever he should evidently make himself known. 'The law and the prophets,' says Christ, 'were until John. Since that the kingdom of God is preached, and every man presseth into it.' The baptism of John and that of Jesus were essentially the same, one into a profession of belief in the Messiah yet to come, and the other into a possession of belief in the Messiah already come.

"Thus John's baptism began to do what his words began to predict, to separate the righteous from the wicked, to prepare the righteous for eternal life, and leave the wicked to the consequences of their sins ; began to establish the kingdom of God, whose initiatory rite was baptism, just as circumcision was the initiatory rite of God's ancient church. Thus the kingdom of God came not with observation. While men were saying, 'Lo here, and lo there,' the kingdom of God was in the midst of them.

"But after all this knowledge of the nature of the kingdom, or Christianity, which was possessed by John the Baptist, and after baptizing Jesus with his own hands, and receiving the Divine testimony of which he had been forewarned, so possessed was he with the Jewish prejudices, of the temporal splendor and power of the

Messiah, and so discouraged by his long imprisonment, that he sent two of his disciples to inquire if he were actually the Messiah. Jesus sent them back to tell all they saw and heard, and to leave him to form his own judgment, adding what throws light on the reasons of John's doubts, 'Blessed is he whoever is not offended in me ; who does not consider the lowliness of my appearance incompatible with the loftiness of my pretentions.'

"This good and holy man, having lived just long enough to see the rising twilight of the new dispensation for which he was sent to prepare the way, fell a victim to the intrigues and revenge of a wicked woman. Herodias, the wife of one of the sons of Herod the Great, accompanying her husband to Rome, there became acquainted with Herod the tetrarch of Perea, and after her return to Judea she abandoned her husband, and with her daughter Salome went to live with him, in open defiance of the laws of God and man. John, the intrepid prophet of righteousness, reproved such flagrant iniquity in high places, and said to the royal transgressor, 'It is not lawful for thee to have her.' For this bold testimony for righteousness he was sent to the castle Machaerus, on the confines of Palestine and Arabia. But the sleepless revenge of Herodias followed him even there, and he died, as is well known, a martyr to the truth. Thus perished John the Baptist, the morning star of Christianity, and his dying eyes caught scarcely a glimpse of the glory that was revealed.

"There is no subject which literature approaches with such diffidence as the personal character and history of Christ. There is no theme on which language is found so inadequate and imperfect. A person in human form, with every attribute of humanity, except sin, exhibiting perfect goodness in combination with infallible wisdom, clothed with extensive power over physical nature, and a knowledge of futurity at once extensive and circumstantial ; the declared end and object of a train of miraculous interpositions running back to the very foundation of the world, himself the beginning and cause of a new order of things, embracing the whole world and all succeeding times; his doctrines destined to sway the minds of the millions of the human race, to form their opinions, to mould their characters, to shape their expectations, to reign in their minds, and judge their actions, to convict and purify their consciences, to cleanse them from sin, and prepare them for his own society and the presence of God in the spiritual world–worthily to speak of such a being is a task before which I confess that my speech falters and my vocabulary seems meagre and inadequate. This difficulty remains whatever view we adopt of his metaphysical rank in the universe. From the fierce controversy as to the nature of Christ, so early raised and which more than any other cause has disturbed its harmony, I am most happy to escape. That belongs to the history of opinions, and volumes on volumes would not contain their endless diversity. What men have thought of the person of Jesus of Nazareth, and what he actually was, and did, and taught, and brought to pass, are two things entirely distinct. The former is a matter of mere speculation, the latter embraces all that is necessary.

"We read of Jesus, that, immediately after his baptism and transfiguration, by John, directed by Divine impulse, he retired into solitude, where he passed forty days in preparation, doubtless, for the great work in which he was about to engage. From this solitary sojourn he returned filled with the Spirit, with that measure of wisdom and knowledge and power which was necessary for his mission to mankind. From that forty days' retirement he came back to the world with a scheme of religion entirely new. It differed from everything that had gone before in being spiritual and universal. Its plan was perfect at first. It was not to grow up, and take such a form as circumstances might dictate ; but with a plastic power, like that of the Divine Mind itself, it was to transform and mould all things according to its unalterable purpose. It is with reference to this fulness of knowledge, by which he was exalted not only above all the prophets which went before him, but all those whom he used as instruments in propagating and establishing his religion, that it is said of him, that 'God giveth not the spirit by measure unto him.' 'The law was given by Moses, but grace and truth came by Jesus Christ.'

"The divine plan being thus communicated to the mind of Christ, it was necessary that he should have the power of carrying it into effect. Having received this divine commission, it was necessary that it should be authenticated. The plan was divine, but such were the ignorance and blindness of mankind that it is not at all probable that the world would have recognized and embraced it as divine, had it not been authenticated by miracles. Mankind, particularly in rude ages, want not only truth but authority–not only truth but the certainty that it is truth–or, not being embraced with sufficient confidence, it will do them no good.

"Jesus returned from his forty days' seclusion possessed of supernatural wisdom, which guarded him from all mistake, and enabled him in all circumstances to say and to do the thing which his present condition required; he came with miraculous knowledge of the manner, for instance, and circumstances of his death, the success of his religion, and the spiritual power to which he was to be exalted. He came with supernatural control over the order of nature, such as is most striking to the unsophisticated understandings of mankind, to persuade them of the connection of its possessor with God. His touch healed the sick, his will changed the elements, his command stilled the tempest, his voice raised the dead. But what was quite as striking to those with whom he associated, he could read men's most secret thoughts, and tell them the transactions of their past lives, and foresee what they were hereafter to do.

"But the system, though perfect in itself, existed nowhere but in his own mind. How was it to be introduced? The human mind was not a blank on which might be written the institutions and principles of the new religion. It was already preoccupied, What was already there could not be annihilated or effaced. How could the new be made to supersede the old? It could not be done at once. It could only be done by degrees, by engrafting the new upon the old where it was practicable, and by infusing into the current of language and thought new principles which might insensibly color the whole mass, thus superseding rather than destroying what was already in existence.

The Jewish religion was already in being, as the

stock upon which to engraft his own. He himself was expected, but in another character from what he could assume. The whole phraseology was in use which designated what he was to accomplish. What would the highest wisdom have dictated him to do? What does the man do who has a house to build, but has an old one already on the spot ? Does he begin by giving it to the flames, or by throwing it all aside ? No ! He selects from it whatever is sound and incorporates it with the new building.

"This was precisely what Jesus did with regard to the religion of the Jews, and the expectations and phraseology which were then in existence as to the Messiah and the new dispensation. To reject them would have made the task of introducing the new religion much more difficult. The only course which wisdom could direct was to adopt the existing phraseology, and give it such a sense as would correspond with his real character and office. The Jews were accustomed to call the Messiah the 'Son of Man,' from the vision of Daniel, in which he saw one like 'the Son of Man,' invested with great power and dignity. He was likewise called the 'Son of God,' from the second Psalm. These appellations he assumed, and by assuming them claimed all that belonged to the Messiah. The Messiah was expected as a king, and the new dispensation as a kingdom. This was not literally a fact, but was spiritually true in a sense transcending the most exalted conceptions of the most bigoted and ambitious Jew. Nor ought it to militate against this view of things, that it may seem to be inconsistent with perfect candor and dealing. No language that he could have used would have given them a clear conception of Christianity, as it actually was to be. Their own phraseology of a kingdom would come as near as any that he could adopt. What it was to be time only could develop. We, who know what it is, acquiesce in the propriety of his use of the Messianic language, as it then existed, giving it at the same time such an interpretation as made it the symbolic expression of the highest spiritual truth.

"To exemplify the principles which I have laid down, to show the wisdom, the miraculous knowledge of Jesus, the full understanding that he had of the whole system from the beginning, and the manner in which he insinuated the glorious and eternal truths of Christianity through the Messianic phraseology of that time, I shall proceed to analyze some of his first discourses.

"The ministry of Jesus began in Galilee, but at what time of the year we are not informed. Of his first tour through that country, in which he attended the marriage-feast at Cana, we have only a general notice. Of his discourses nothing now remains but their commencing sentence : 'Repent, for the kingdom of God is at hand.' Multitudes soon gathered around him, and his fame spread throughout all Syria.

"His first recorded discourse is that which he held with Nicodemus at Jerusalem, at the first passover which occurred after the commencement of his ministry. This conversation introduces to us one of the most interesting scenes of the New Testament. It presents us a practical proof of that miraculous wisdom with which Christ was endowed, which made him equally at home with the learned, acute, and experienced member of the Jewish Senate at Jerusalem, and the humble, simple peasants and fishermen of Galilee. 'And it came to pass when he was in Jerusalem, at the Passover on the feastday, many believed on his name when they saw the miracles that he did.' 'Marvel not that I said unto thee, ye must be born again. The wind bloweth whither it listeth, and thou hearest the sound thereof, but canst not tell whence it cometh, and whither it goeth ; so is everyone that is born of the Spirit.' Spiritual birth, true religion, is not confined, as you Jews suppose, to one tribe or family. It is as free as air, and the kingdom of God, which you expect to be a national thing, will spread over the earth as that does, without any regard to the boundaries of nations and kindreds. Its empire is the soul, everywhere free, everyone capable of receiving it, not more in those whose material bodies have descended from Abraham than those who have never heard of his name. If you really desire, then, to enter into the kingdom of God, to be my disciple, come not here by night, go openly and be baptized. Be a Christian, not outwardly alone, but inwardly; hear my doctrines, receive my spirit, and trust no more to your descent from Abraham. In the course of the conversation, he glances at two other facts no less offensive to the Jewish prejudices of Nicodemus, the crucifixion of the Messiah and the extension of his kingdom to the gentiles. 'As Moses lifted up the serpent in the wilderness, even so must the Son of Man be lifted up, that whosoever believeth on him should not perish, but have everlasting life. For God sent His Son into the world, not to condemn the world,' not to destroy the nations as you Jews suppose, 'but that through him the world might be saved.' Such was the transcendent wisdom of the Saviour, from the very commencement of his mission. Before the wisdom of this youthful teacher, learning and age and experience were overborne and subdued, and Nicodemus must have retired convinced no less by his discourses than his miracles that he was a teacher come from God.

"Soon after this conversation Jesus returned into Galilee, and, passing through Samaria, held that remarkable discourse with the woman of Samaria at the well of Jacob, which I have noticed in a former letter.

"On his arrival at Nazareth, his previous residence, he attempted to preach in the synagogue where he had been accustomed to worship. The people listened to the first part of his discourse with pleasure and admiration, though, according to a strong propensity of human nature, they were disposed to sneer at him as the son of a carpenter. At the first hint, however, of the doctrine that the new dispensation was not to be a national religion, but to be extended to gentile as well as Jew, they became violently enraged. They might have been led to suspect that he was not altogether sound in the national faith of a Messiah who was to destroy the heathen, from his manner of quoting that striking passage of Isaiah, 'The spirit of the Lord is upon me, because he hath anointed me to preach glad tidings to the poor; he hath sent me to heal the broken-hearted, to preach deliverance to the captives and recovery of sight to the blind ; to set at liberty them that are bound, to preach the acceptable year of the Lord;' —here he stopped. The rest of the sentence is, 'and the day of vengeance of our God.' Had he quoted the rest of the sentence without explanation, as applicable to himself, they would have understood him to sanction their expectation that he was to destroy and not to save the other nations of the earth, and cried out, perhaps, Hosanna to the son of David ! But not only did he pass over this most important part of their Messianic traditions, so comforting to them under their present political oppression, but he went on to intimate that the heathen were not only to be spared, but to be admitted into the kingdom of the Messiah. 'I tell you of a truth, many widows were in Israel in the days of Elias, but unto none of them was Elias sent save unto Sarepta, a city of Sidon, unto a woman that was a widow. And many lepers were in Israel in the days of Eliseus the prophet, and none of them were cleansed saving Naaman the Syrian.' This was too much. A Messiah who could tolerate or look favorably upon the heathen, was not to be endured. 'And all they in the synagogue, when they heard these things, were filled with wrath, and rose up and thrust him out of the city, and led him to the brow of the hill whereon the city was built, that they might cast him down headlong. But he, passing through the midst of them, went his way, and came down to Capernaum, a city of Galilee, and taught them on the Sabbath day

"The fame of his miracles and his doctrines went on to increase, till the synagogues became too small to contain the crowds which flocked to hear him. He began, therefore, to teach them in the open air. Once he preached to them from a ship, while they stood on the shore ; once from a rising ground, that his voice might be better heard by so vast a multitude. His discourse on this occasion is denominated, from the place where it was delivered, the Sermon on the Mount. Let us examine its contents, and mark the wonderful wisdom which it displays, couching eternal truths in language precisely adapted to present circumstances; so that the Jew, when he heard it, was cured of his errors, and the Christian to all times finds himself edified, as if it had been addressed to him alone. In that vast multitude which was assembled from all parts of Judea, there were, it is probable, men of all the different sentiments which were cherished by the Jewish people at that period, uniting in but one common sentiment, that the Messiah should be a temporal deliverer, should cleanse Jerusalem and the holy land of the Roman standards which were perched on every tower, and redeem the people of God from the degrading tribute they were yearly compelled to pay. They were ready to take up arms in the holy cause of patriotism and religion. They wanted but the signal of his hand to take up their line of march to the city of David, and there they supposed that he would stand highest in the new monarchy whose sword had drank most freely of the blood of the slain. They collected about him with hearts bursting with national pride and ambition. What must have been their astonishment and disappointment when the first sentence fell from his lips, 'Blessed are the poor in spirit, for theirs is the kingdom of heaven.' The kingdom of God which you have been so long expecting is not an empire of war and conquest, nor is it that of the Jews, to be exercised over foreign nations. It belongs to the humble, the quiet, the contented. It does not come as a cure for outward misfortunes, for political evils, for the relief of proud hearts rankling under oppression, but it speaks comfort to those who are bowed down under the sorrows of life; 'Blessed are they who mourn, for they shall be comforted.' You expect the Messiah to vindicate the weak against the strong, to repel injury, to revenge insult, that he will set up his empire with the sword and defend it by the sword. 'But I say unto you, blessed are the meek, for they shall inherit the earth.' The gentle are those who are to flourish in the days of the Messiah. They shall delight themselves in the abundance of peace. You come to me expecting a sign from heaven, to be fed with manna from the skies, as your fathers were in the desert. I can promise you nothing of the kind. The blessings of my kingdom belong to those only who hunger and thirst after righteousness, for they shall be filled. You expect under the Messiah a reign of bitterness and vengeance, that he will rule with a rod of iron, and dash his enemies in pieces like a potter's vessel. But I come to pronounce blessings on the merciful, for I assure them that they shall find mercy from their eternal Judge. You, who observe the laws of Moses, submit to innumerable ceremonial ablutions, and therefore imagine yourselves pure and prepared for the kingdom of God. I assure you that no such purification will be of any avail in that kingdom ; 'Blessed are the pure in heart, for they shall see God.' The remedies which you propose for mortal ills are essentially defective. You imagine that they can be cured by violence and resentment, that evil may be remedied by evil, instead of being overcome with good. But I say unto you, 'Blessed are the peace-makers, for they shall be called the children of God.' They shall share the blessings of the new dispensation, not those who are vindictive and resentful; but 'Blessed are those who are persecuted for righteousness' sake.'

"The new religion which Jesus was sent to teach was not only to be preached by himself to that generation, but to be perpetuated to all time. His own ministry he knew was to be short, and to have a tragical end. It could be perpetuated in no other way than by choosing assistants while he lived, and training them to take up the work where he laid it down, to receive the gospel from his lips, proclaim it to the world, and when their days should be numbered commit it to others, who should be prepared in their turn to instruct a new generation, and thus send it down to all future times. Had there been no organization of this kind, had Jesus chosen no Apostles, Christianity would have perished on the very threshold of its existence. Accordingly, not long after the commencement of his mission, after a night of prayer to God, doubtless for Divine guidance and direction, he choose twelve men of his more immediate followers, and ordained them as his assistants and successors in the propagation of the new faith. To them he explained more fully the principles of his religion, which to the multitude, for fear of popular commotion, he veiled under the dress of parable and allegory. He sent them during his own ministry as heralds of his approach, to prepare the minds of the people by their own instructions for his more perfect teaching.

"These twelve Apostles were men from the lower orders of society, of but slender literary and intellectual cultivation, without wealth or influential connections. They brought no accession of strength or respectability to his cause. It may seem at first utterly unaccountable on any principle of human policy that he should have made such a selection, and quite as unaccountable that he himself should have chosen to pass through his ministry under an exterior so exceedingly humble; that he should, in the language of the Apostles, have made himself of no reputation, and to all external appearances taken the form of a slave ; but when we reflect upon it, we find that it was dictated by the highest wisdom. His external humility only puts in strong contrast his moral and spiritual glory. He was really so great that nothing external could add to the grandeur of his character. The fact that, without availing himself of a single external advantage, he established a religion which disappointed the hopes of his own nation and offered no bribe to any of the passions to which the ambitious appeal with so much success–that he told his followers from the first that they were to reap no worldly advantage from their connection with him–that his disciples were utterly destitute of those acquirements by which any cause is usually carried forward–all these things throw the philosophical back upon the only success, the reality of his mission from God, the moral power which truth always carries with it, and those miracalous attestations which are strongest evidence to the unsophisticated mind of man of a mission from the Most High.

"It may at first sight seem strange, when he might have gone up to Jerusalem and chosen his disciples from the most learned, gifted, and accomplished of the rabbinical schools which were then flourishing there, that he should have made such a choice. Over them he would have manifested the same immeasurable superiority, and might have wielded them to accomplish his purposes as easily as those humbler persons whom he actually choose as his companions. Between him and the intellectual and cultivated there would seem to have been a closer sympathy than with those uneducated Galileans who, as far as we at this time are able to see, were mere children in his presence. But this arrangement, like every other, was founded in the highest wisdom. The function which they were appointed to fill did not call either for great talents or for extensive learning. They were to originate nothing, they were to add nothing to what he had taught. Their office was simply that of witnesses of what he had said and done and suffered. 'And ye also shall bear witness,' said he to his disciples, 'because ye have been with me from the beginning.' After his resurrection he said to them : 'Thus it is written, and thus it behooved the Messiah to suffer, and to rise from the dead the third day, and that repentance and remission of sins should be preached in his name among all nations, beginning at Jerusalem. And ye are witnesses of these things. Ye shall receive power after that the Holy Ghost is come upon you, and ye shall be witnesses unto me, both in Jerusalem and in all Judea, and in Samaria, and unto the uttermost parts of the earth.'

"This being the office of the disciples, intellectual cultivation was not a necessary requisite. The qualities most necessary to a witness are simplicity, integrity, and courage. Through them the world had received the Gospel. The more transparent the medium through which we receive it, the less coloring it takes from the minds through which it was transmitted. The consequence is that we have the most simple and childlike narrative that the world has ever read. We do not see the historians at all. All we see is Jesus Christ, his doctrine, his character, his life, his miracles. There is no attempt at the introduction of the philosophy or opinions of the times, with the exception of the beginning of the Gospel of John ; and it is unnecessary to say that those lines have created more controversy in the Christian Church than all the rest of the letters. What Jesus wanted of his Apostles was principally to be his witnesses to the world and to all succeeding ages. On their testimony, in fact, the faith of the successive millions of the Christian Church has depended. The Gospels are nothing more nor less than their testimony. Jesus himself left nothing written. All that we know either of him or his doctrines we receive through them. Without their testimony we would not know that such a person had ever existed. Without their testimony we would not know what he taught or how he lived. It was on the strength of what they have seen and heard that they claimed to be the religious teachers of the world. The relation which the Apostles understood themselves to sustain to Jesus as witnesses is fully and clearly brought out in Peter's speech to Cornelius and his friends: 'How God anointed Jesus of Nazareth with the Holy Ghost and with power, who went about doing good, and healing all that were oppressed of the devil, for God was with him. And we are witnesses of all things which he did both in the land of the Jews and Jerusalem, whom they slew and hanged on a tree, him God raised up the third day, and showed him openly, not to all the people, but unto witnesses chosen before of God, even to us, who did eat and drink with him after he rose from the dead.'

"When the Saviour bowed his head upon the cross, and said, ' It is finished,' the Gospel was complete. He had discharged his office as a teacher. Nothing could be added to it, and nothing could be taken from it. The system was perfect. The duty of the Apostles was to promulgate it to the world. So you will observe that the promise of Divine assistance, as far as doctrines are concerned, goes no further than strengthening their memories ; 'But the Comforter, which is the Holy Ghost, which the Father will send in my name, he shall teach you all things, and bring all things to your remembrance whatsoever I have said unto you.' They were occasionally instructed what to do, but never, that we read of, to preach any new doctrine which had not been taught by Christ himself.

"It may seem strange to those who are accustomed to dispute about words and phrases, that Christ should have left nothing written, nothing which we can identify as the very words which he spoke. The stickler for creeds and formulas may lament that all the disputes of after ages were not anticipated and prevented by a written declaration of the Saviour, which would have been so plain that no dulness could have misapprehended, no ingenuity perverted it. We are fully justified, I believe, in asserting that no such precaution would have been effectual. Human language is essentially ambiguous, every word having a variety of significations, any one of which becomes probable only because it better suits the connection, the purpose, or the sentiments of the writer. Language is always addressed to reasonable beings, and it is necessary for them to exercise their reason in order to understand it. It is so with Christ's plainest instructions. We are always obliged to use our reason in order to decide in what sense his words are to be taken. When he tells us, 'If any man come to me, and hate not his father and mother, and wife and children, and brethren and sisters, yea, and his own life also, he cannot be my disciple;' are we to interpret this literally, and say that no man can be a Christian without hating father and mother, and sisters and brothers? By no means. And why ? Because it is not reasonable to believe that such was his meaning. We cannot suppose that Christ intended his followers to prove false to the most important relations we sustain in this life. We conclude, therefore, that he did not use the word hate in a literal, but a figurative sense of loving them less than himself and his cause. So we interpret the precept which commands us to cut off a right hand or pluck out a right eye. We do not cut off our hands and pluck out our eyes, not because we are not literally commanded to do so, but reason teaches us that he did not mean literally to be so taken. So whatever Christ might have left written, there would have remained the same difficulty of interpretation. We should still he obliged to rest on probability, just as we do now. We cannot be infallibly certain that we take a sentence of Scripture in the true sense, without possessing inspiration ourselves. We cannot know that we are inspired, without the power of miracles, or unless some miracle were wrought for our sakes, for otherwise we could not have distinguished those thoughts which were miraculously suggested from those which occurred in the ordinary operations of our minds.

"Then, even had the Saviour left the Gospel written with his own hand, we would still have been compelled to rely on human testimony that the same identical words were preserved. The thing, then, is evidently better as it is. We would have been compelled at last to rely on human testimony as to what Christ did and taught and suffered. What more competent witnesses could we possibly have than those who were with him on terms of the greatest familiarity during his whole ministry ? In what better form could we have this testimony than in the Gospel according to Matthew, written by one of those who were with him from the beginning, and who was present at his crucifixion, who ate and drank with him after he rose from the dead, and who spent his life in propagating his religion? What more unobjectionable testimony than that of John, who had been one of the disciples of John the Baptist, who saw the transfiguration, leaned on his bosom, and shared his most intimate friendship ? As collateral proof, what more authentic than the memoirs of Luke and Mark, who were the constant companions of the Apostles, and heard them rehearse over and over the wonderful story of the teachings and miracles of Jesus?

"Considered in this light, as human testimony, and it is the only light in which they can he regarded, those who understand the principles of evidence most thoroughly tell us that their evidence is the more weighty and satisfactory from their slight variations from each other. Those who frequent courts of justice tell us that it is utterly vain to expect entire consistency of a number of witnesses, let them be ever so honest and ever so competent. Agreement in the main facts is all that is expected, and nothing will sooner cause suspicion of collusion than for two witnesses to make, word for word, the same statement. No human being ever told the same story twice in the same words and in the same order.

Nothing can he more evident than that the historians were subjected to the same common laws which govern the operations of the human mind. We have in the letter three different relations of Paul's vision and conversion, twice by himself in public speeches, and one from the letter of Luke, probably from his own lips in private conversation. Yet the three accounts all vary from each other in words and circumstances. The four Evangelists all give us the inscription upon the cross of Jesus, yet no two agree in the precise form of words which was used. Matthew says that the accusation was, 'This is Jesus, the king of the Jews.' Mark says that the superscription was, 'The king of the Jews.' Luke says it was, 'This is the king of the Jews.' John says that the title on his cross was, 'Jesus of Nazareth, the king of the Jews.' Here, then, is a variation in the testimony. It is impossible that more than one of these inscriptions can he verbally accurate. But it creates no distrust, and not one in a hundred of the Christian church has been aware of its existence. It is an immaterial variation, a discrepancy which must, always be allowed in human testimony, and nothing could he more unreasonable or absurd than to allow the least shade of doubt to pass over the mind as to the reality of the inscription because of this verbal discrepancy. The first three Evangelists have given us Christ's prayer in his agony at the garden of Gethsemane, but each of them in different words. Yet no man in his sober senses would think of doubting the actual occurrence of that thrilling scene on that account. If anything in all history of the past can he said to hear the native impress of truth, it is this whole transaction."

A BLOOD COVENANT IS THE MOST SOLEMN, BINDING AGREEMENT POSSIBLE BETWEEN TWO PARTIES.

Perhaps one of the least understood, and yet most important and relevant factors necessary for an appreciation of the series of covenants and covenant relationships that our God has chosen to employ in His dealings with man, is the concept of the BLOOD COVENANT!

In this volume which has been "sold out," and "unavailable" for generations, lies truth which has blessed and will continue to bless every pastor, teacher, every serious Christian desiring to "go on with God."

Andrew Murray stated it beautifully years ago, when he said that if we were to but grasp the full knowledge of what God desires to do for us and understood the nature of His promises, it would "make the Covenant the very gate of heaven! May the Holy Spirit give us some vision of its glory."

$10.95 + 2.00 postage and handling

THE HEAVENS DECLARE . . .
William D. Banks

More than 250 pages!
More than 50 illustrations!

- Who named the stars and why?
- What were the original names of the stars?
- What is the secret message hidden in the stars?

The surprising, **secret message** contained in the earliest, original names of the stars, is revealed in this new book.

The deciphering of the star names provides a fresh revelation from the heart of **the intelligence** behind creation. Ten years of research includes material from the British Museum dating prior to 2700 B.C.

A clear explanation is given showing that early man had a sophisticated knowledge of One, True God!

$6.95 + $1.50 Shipping/Handling

ALIVE AGAIN!
William D. Banks

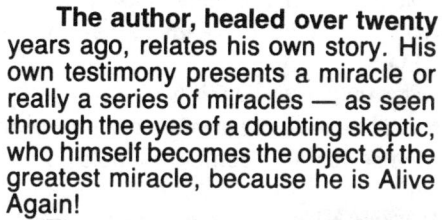

Bill Banks:
Terminal Cancer:
48 hours to live.
Miraculously healed!

The author, healed over twenty years ago, relates his own story. His own testimony presents a miracle or really a series of miracles — as seen through the eyes of a doubting skeptic, who himself becomes the object of the greatest miracle, because he is Alive Again!

The way this family pursues and finds divine healing as well as a great spiritual blessing provides a story that will at once bless you, refresh you, restore your faith or challenge it! You will not be the same after you have read this true account of the healing gospel of Jesus Christ, and how He is working in the world today.

The healing message contained in this book needs to be heard by every cancer patient, every seriously ill person, and by every Christian hungering for the reality of God.

More than a powerful testimony — here is teaching which can introduce you or those whom you love to healing and to a new life in the Spirit!

$4.95 + $1.50 Shipping/Handling

POWERFUL NEW BOOK

MINISTERING TO ABORTION'S AFTERMATH

Bill and Sue Banks

This new book is unique because it offers real help for the suffering women who have already had abortions. This book is full of GOOD NEWS!

It shows how to minister to them, or may be used by the women themselves as it contains simple steps to self-ministry.

Millions of women **have had abortions**: every one of them is a potential candidate for the type of ministry presented in this book. Every minister, every counsellor, every Christian should be familiar with these truths which can set people free.

$5.95 + $1.50 Shipping/Handling

Impact Christian Books, Inc.
332 Leffingwell Avenue, Suite 101
Kirkwood, MO 63122

EXCITING NEW BOOK
ANSWERS AGE-OLD QUESTION

How to Tap Into the Wisdom of God
By William D. Banks

The author draws upon the Scriptural patterns and keys established by the Prophet Daniel to present readily understandable methods any believer can employ to *Tap into the Wisdom of God*. He shows from Scripture that it is both God's intention and will for man to turn to Him as the Source of knowledge.

You will learn seven major keys to receiving knowledge and find at least twenty-one practical encouragements to build your faith to seek God for answers.

Plus a Revelation

Discover for yourself the fascinating and prophetic secrets contained in Daniel Chapter Six, presented in the ninth chapter of this book. Chapter nine, which is actually a bonus book, presents an apparently undiscovered revelation showing more than one hundred parallels between Daniel and Jesus Christ.

"The most exciting thing I discovered was that what God did for Daniel, He can do for any believer!"
P.M., Bible Teacher, Kansas.

$10.95 + $1.50 Shipping

Impact Christian Books, Inc.
332 Leffingwell Ave., Suite 101,
Kirkwood, MO 63122

FOR ADDITIONAL COPIES WRITE:

Impactian Christian Books

332 Leffingwell Ave., Suite 101
Kirkwood, MO 63122

AVAILABLE AT YOUR LOCAL BOOKSTORE, OR YOU MAY ORDER DIRECTLY. Toll-Free, order-line only M/C, DISC, or VISA 1-800-451-2708.